PSYCHOLOGY OF ALTRUISM

PSYCHOLOGY OF EMOTIONS, MOTIVATIONS AND ACTIONS

Additional books in this series can be found on Nova's website under the Series tab.

Additional e-books in this series can be found on Nova's website under the e-book tab.

PSYCHOLOGY OF EMOTIONS, MOTIVATIONS AND ACTIONS

PSYCHOLOGY OF ALTRUISM

HELENA KOPPEL
EDITOR

New York

For permission to use material from this book please contact us:
Telephone 631-231-7269; Fax 631-231-8175
Web Site: http://www.novapublishers.com

NOTICE TO THE READER

The Publisher has taken reasonable care in the preparation of this book, but makes no expressed or implied warranty of any kind and assumes no responsibility for any errors or omissions. No liability is assumed for incidental or consequential damages in connection with or arising out of information contained in this book. The Publisher shall not be liable for any special, consequential, or exemplary damages resulting, in whole or in part, from the readers' use of, or reliance upon, this material. Any parts of this book based on government reports are so indicated and copyright is claimed for those parts to the extent applicable to compilations of such works.

Independent verification should be sought for any data, advice or recommendations contained in this book. In addition, no responsibility is assumed by the publisher for any injury and/or damage to persons or property arising from any methods, products, instructions, ideas or otherwise contained in this publication.

This publication is designed to provide accurate and authoritative information with regard to the subject matter covered herein. It is sold with the clear understanding that the Publisher is not engaged in rendering legal or any other professional services. If legal or any other expert assistance is required, the services of a competent person should be sought. FROM A DECLARATION OF PARTICIPANTS JOINTLY ADOPTED BY A COMMITTEE OF THE AMERICAN BAR ASSOCIATION AND A COMMITTEE OF PUBLISHERS.

Additional color graphics may be available in the e-book version of this book.

LIBRARY OF CONGRESS CATALOGING-IN-PUBLICATION DATA

Psychology of altruism / editor, Helena Koppel.
     pages cm
  Includes index.
  ISBN 978-1-62808-152-7 (soft cover)
  1. Altruism--Psychological aspects. I. Koppel, Helena.
  BF637.H4P877 2013
  155.2'32--dc23
                        2013019808

Published by Nova Science Publishers, Inc. † New York

CONTENTS

PREFACE

In this book the authors present current research in the study of the psychology of altruism. Topics discussed include the psychology of altruism as it relates to the problems of mechanism, egoism, and determinism; the evolution of feeling; and altruism and economic growth in an institutional theoretical perspective.

Chapter 1 – Although a plethora of explanatory models, constructs, hypotheses, and experimental studies have been offered by psychologists to explain altruism, there has been, thus far, no general consensus as to what exactly altruism is, how it comes about, or how best to study it. The authors contend that this confusion about the nature and meaning of altruism stems from the way in which it has been conceptualized and investigated. In particular, they argue that pre-investigatory philosophical commitments to mechanism, egoism, and necessary determinism have led many researchers to define, study, and explain altruism in ways that not only fail to provide adequate understanding of it, but which also destroy its inherently meaningful nature. In particular, the authors show that the presumptions of mechanism, egoism, and necessary determinism lead psychologists to advance and embrace less parsimonious explanations of altruism than otherwise might be possible, as well as force them to engage the question of altruism in ways that ultimately do not so much explain the phenomenon as explain it away. Briefly, by way of alternative, the authors discuss some possible conceptual and methodological solutions to the problems inherent in traditional approaches to the study of human altruism that avoid the problems of mechanism, egoism, and determinism.

Chapter 2 – There has been a great deal of interest lately in "evolutionary psychology" as it relates to human moral psychology and other aspects of human thought and culture. The present chapter considers how morality seen as depending on altruism and on empathy as essential to such altruism might conceivably have evolved. This will require some evolutionary speculation, but also a great deal of conceptual analysis. We have to consider how empathy helps to make altruism possible, but also how evolution could have moved toward empathic creatures via a series of steps each of which had survival value. It will be argued, among other things, that an instinct for proximity helps produce creatures who are open to mutual empathic influence, and also that instincts of imitation (loosely understood) serve to bridge the gap between proximity (flocking, herding) and full-blown empathy. The role of mirror neurons in all this will be considered, as will the usefulness of mammalian mothering as a basis for a kind of generalized human sympathy that has evolutionary survival value.

Chapter 3 – This paper aims to explore the links existing between altruism and economic growth, within an Institutionalist theoretical framework. The different notions of altruism will first be scrutinized, and the works of Thorstein Veblen and Gunnar Myrdal will be used in order to show that pro-social attitudes can play a significant role in driving economic growth, both on the supply and demand side.

In: Psychology of Altruism   ISBN: 978-1-62808-152-7
Editor: Helena Koppel   © 2013 Nova Science Publishers, Inc.

Chapter 1

THE PSYCHOLOGY OF ALTRUISM AND THE PROBLEMS OF MECHANISM, EGOISM, AND DETERMINISM

Edwin E. Gantt, Jeffrey S. Reber and Jordan D. Hyde*

Brigham Young University, Provo, Utah, US

ABSTRACT

Although a plethora of explanatory models, constructs, hypotheses, and experimental studies have been offered by psychologists to explain altruism, there has been, thus far, no general consensus as to what exactly altruism is, how it comes about, or how best to study it. We contend that this confusion about the nature and meaning of altruism stems from the way in which it has been conceptualized and investigated. In particular, we argue that pre-investigatory philosophical commitments to mechanism, egoism, and necessary determinism have led many researchers to define, study, and explain altruism in ways that not only fail to provide adequate understanding of it, but which also destroy its inherently meaningful nature. In particular, we show that the presumptions of mechanism, egoism, and necessary determinism lead psychologists to advance and embrace less parsimonious explanations of

---

* Corresponding author: Edwin E. Gantt, Department of Psychology, Brigham Young University, 1086 SWKT, Provo, UT 84602, US. E-mail: ed_gantt@byu.edu.

altruism than otherwise might be possible, as well as force them to engage the question of altruism in ways that ultimately do not so much explain the phenomenon as explain it away. Briefly, by way of alternative, we discuss some possible conceptual and methodological solutions to the problems inherent in traditional approaches to the study of human altruism that avoid the problems of mechanism, egoism, and determinism.

THE PSYCHOLOGY OF ALTRUISM AND THE PROBLEMS OF MECHANISM, EGOISM, AND DETERMINISM

"I did not ask myself, Should I do this? But, How will I do this? Every step of my childhood had brought me to this crossroads. I must take the right path, or I would no longer be myself." (Irene Gut Opdyke, 1999, p. 126)

By the spring of 1942, Irene Gut, a young Catholic girl living in Poland during the Nazi occupation, had already suffered a great many of the horrors of war.[1] During the Russian invasion of 1939, and the subsequent brutal "Sovietizing" of her homeland following the decision by Hitler and Stalin to "partition" Poland, Irene was a seventeen year-old nursing student away from home for the first time. Unfortunately, while caring for injured Polish soldiers, she became caught up in the fighting and was physically and sexually assaulted by several Red Army soldiers who then left her to die in the snow. Later, trying to make her way back home, she was arrested, imprisoned, and tortured by Soviet authorities who suspected her of being affiliated with partisan forces. In time, however, she escaped and was able to make her way back home – which was now firmly under German control.

Although the Russian presence in Poland was replaced by the presumably "more civilized" forces of Hitler's Germany, Irene knew that it was best for her to keep as low a profile as possible and pray that she be left alone. Despite her best efforts to avoid drawing any unwanted attention, however, Irene was seized one Sunday by German soldiers as she left church, and she and a friend were forced into slave labor at a nearby munitions plant. During an inspection of the plant, Irene caught the eye of an older German Major who was

---

[1] Irene's story is told at much greater length in both her 1999 autobiography, *In My Hands: Memories of a Holocaust Rescuer*, and in the interviews recorded in Kristen Renwick Monroe's 2004 book, *The Hands of Compassion: Portraits of Moral Choice during the Holocaust*. The brief quote that begins this chapter is taken from Irene's autobiography (p. 126).

conducting the inspection. He took pity on her situation and, seemingly genuinely concerned for her welfare, secured her immediate release from the munitions factory. Further, he saw to it that she was hired as a cook and a waitress at a nearby hotel restaurant that catered to German officers in the Wehrmacht.

The hotel where Irene worked was near a Jewish ghetto and, on her way home from work each night, Irene often walked along the wall that separated the ghetto from the rest of the town. Knowing that the people on the other side were starving and suffering, Irene made a bold decision, one that was punishable by torture and death if she were discovered. At the end of each workday, Irene would sneak food out of the hotel kitchen and on her way home she would toss the bundles of stolen food over the wall to the desperate people waiting on the other side. After all she had been through already in her young life, Irene felt that she simply could not just stand by and do nothing when there were others in need. She had to do something to help. And, with time and opportunity, Irene did help, and in many courageous ways. She was able to secure jobs for a number of ghetto residents in her kitchen and eventually helped them escape the ghetto just as it was being liquidated.

On the day of the liquidation, in the dark of night, Irene snuck several Jews into the basement of the German Major's new villa where she had recently been hired to serve as his personal maid and cook. She hid several more of them in the forest outside of town and made regular trips out to the forest with food and supplies to sustain the people that were hiding there. She did all of this at great personal risk, all the while knowing that if she was ever caught not only would she be executed, but in accord with Nazi policy all of her family would be executed as well. Almost on a daily basis she put herself and her loved ones at great risk for people who were initially complete strangers to her.

One day, after a visit to the market to purchase some groceries, Irene (along with all the other Poles in the town at that time) was forced to witness the hanging of a Jewish family, as well as the Polish family that had been hiding them from the authorities. Even the smallest infant children of the families were not spared the cruelties of Nazi justice. Irene was so upset by this terrible event that when she returned to the Major's villa she forgot to lock the door from the inside and leave the key in the lock, a precaution that she had always taken before so that she would be alerted if the Major were unexpectedly to come home. As Irene entered the kitchen four of the Jews who were hiding in the cellar crept up to meet with her. As Irene shared the horror of what had happened in the market that morning they tried desperately to calm and reassure her, but the Major, who had come home earlier than usual that day, walked into the kitchen and immediately saw Irene surrounded by the Jews she had been hiding. Furious at Irene's betrayal, the Major retired to his study to decide the fates of Irene, her Jewish friends, and, ultimately, Irene's family. Though the Major was quite fond of Irene, and was unlikely to turn her in, he could not tolerate Jews being hidden in his house and would, therefore, either opt to throw them out on the street or turn them over to the Gestapo for "processing."

Facing these very real and very terrible possibilities, Irene made an unbelievably difficult and heart-wrenching decision in that moment of extremity. She decided to go to the Major and plead for her friends, to offer herself up to be punished in their place if only they would be set free. Drunk and angry, the 70 year-old German officer refused Irene's pleas, instead offering her his promise of silence in return for her willingness to be his mistress and "give an old man the last joy in his life" (Monroe, 2004, p. 162). Irene agreed to the bargain and the Jews she was hiding remained safe in the villa until the end of the war.

As a devout Catholic, it was very important to Irene to clear her conscience with a priest to be sure that God would approve of the reasons for her choices and forgive her actions. She went to see her priest to confess to him what she was doing and why. However, far from granting God's blessing or forgiveness, the priest informed her that she was committing a grievous sin by sleeping with the Major and that she must immediately stop what she was doing or her soul would be eternally damned. Moreover, he urged her to turn in the Jews she was hiding and told her that if she did not do so she would never be able to find peace with God. Irene walked out of the church that day, never to return to another church in her life, choosing instead to protect the lives of her friends even over her own promise of eternal life. By the end of the war, Irene rescued all 12 of the Jews who lived in the Major's cellar, as well as several more who were hiding in the woods. The Israeli Holocaust Commission later named her one of the "Righteous Among the Nations" and awarded her the Yad Vashem medal for the lives she saved during the war. Yet, despite all she had done and the accolades that ensued, Irene, like so many other people who appear to act altruistically, claims there was nothing extraordinary or particularly heroic about what she did. As another Holocaust rescuer responded when asked about his decision to save several Jews: "I don't think that I did anything that special. I think what I did was what everybody normally should be doing" (Monroe, 1996, p. 210). Or, as yet another rescuer said: "I have to help those in need, and when people need help, you have to do it" (Monroe, 2004, p. 101).

THE PSYCHOLOGICAL STUDY OF ALTRUISM

While, in reality, only a relatively tiny percentage of people in the occupied countries of Europe did what Irene did, there are enough examples of rescuers of Jews in Europe as well as other examples of people acting in what appear to be genuinely selfless ways (e.g., Mother Teresa) that psychologists have been compelled to take up the possibility of genuine altruism as a topic of research. Indeed, ignoring this possible motivation would likely result in an incomplete and, potentially misleading, account of human thoughts, feelings, and behaviors. Thus, following the Second World War, a large number of psychologists and other social scientists have conducted numerous studies investigating a motive that seems to operate in at least some people some of the time (see, e.g., Batson, 1991, 2011; Batson and Powell, 2003; Cialdini, Baumann, and Kenrick, 1981; Flescher and Worthen, 2007; Kitzrow, 1999; Monroe, 1996; Post, 2002; Rushton and Sorretino, 1981; Schroeder, Penner, Dovidio, and Piliavin, 1995; Scott and Seglow, 2007; Sober and Wilson, 1998), and which hints in powerful ways at something about us that is profoundly, even perhaps uniquely, human.

Sadly, however, it often seems the case that those experiences that are considered to be most definitively human become less and less clearly understood once psychologists undertake formal scientific study of them. We believe that altruism may well be among the best examples of just such a paradox. Even though, as Scott and Seglow (2007) observe, "Altruism is a simple idea" (p. 1), it is nonetheless one that psychologists have been hard-pressed to conceptualize in a clear and definitive manner, much less study in a focused, unified, or productive way. It has long been noted that most psychological accounts of altruism not only fail to provide a coherent understanding of the phenomenon, but that most such accounts accomplish little more than to obscure it or explain it away (see, e.g., Gantt and Burton, 2013; Gantt and Reber, 1999; Haski-Leventhal, 2009; Kohn, 1990; Kunz, 1998; Monroe, 1996, 2002; Wallach and Wallach, 1983). As noted altruism researcher, Kristen Renwick Monroe (1994) famously observed: "Traditional explanations of altruism resemble a fat lady in a corset; the overall effect may be aesthetically pleasing, but it does fundamental distortion to the underlying reality" (p. 861).

Monroe (1994) notes further that the extensive literature on altruism is so fraught with disagreements over how to define and operationalize it that the result is "widespread confusion in our discussions of altruism" (p. 862), rather than clarification or explanation. Surveying the literature one finds that "altruism can refer to giving, sharing, cooperating, helping, and different forms of other-directed behavior" (Monroe, 1994, p. 862; see also Batson, 2011). In the end, Monroe (2002) has also noted, we are faced with a situation in which "a study that draws conclusions about altruism based on how two-year-olds share toys speaks only tangentially to a study of altruism as conceptualized and operationalized by cooperation among ants or the allocation of family resources among charities and kin" (p. 107). And this situation is only compounded by the fact that altruism as studied in the laboratory quite likely differs in many important ways from altruism as we find it and experience it in the real world of daily life.

One might hope that in the intervening years since Monroe wrote this that some measure of coherence or uniformity might have emerged in the field. Unfortunately, despite some interesting, encouraging, and occasionally counter-intuitive findings over the years, little real conceptual progress seems to have been made toward understanding, explaining or effectively nurturing altruism. Indeed, after exhaustively reviewing the psychological research literature on altruism dating from the early 1960s to the present, Batson and Powell's (2003) concluding summary offers little more about the nature and meaning of altruism than what was already well-known, namely that "in addition to our all-too-apparent failing and fallibilities, we humans are, at times, capable of caring, and caring deeply, for people and issues other than ourselves" (p. 479). Thus, it seems that not only has progress toward achieving a fruitful psychological understanding of altruism been slow in coming, primarily due to persistent conceptual confusions and conflicts over method but that after more than fifty years of careful empirical and theoretical work in the area we seem to have learned little more than what everyone already knew about human beings in the first place.

How is it that more than five decades of intense research and theorizing about altruism have yielded so little additional understanding of its nature, its origins, and its meaning? To answer this question it is necessary, we believe, to understand the process of psychological research and the assumptions that guide it. Specifically, we will show how the assumption of mechanism leads to stagnation in the field of psychology and distraction from the phenomenon under investigation, how the assumption of egoism leads to less empirical and parsimonious explanations, and how the assumption of necessary determinism necessitates an excess of complicated causal explanations and undermines the inherent meaning of altruism.

The Problem of Mechanism

This section focuses specifically on the disciplinary assumption that psychological mechanisms underlie and explain the psychological phenomena and events people experience. Using cognition as an example, we first describe the typical process by which psychological researchers move from an initial interest in a phenomenon (e.g., thinking) that captures their attention to testing hypotheses about the psychological mechanisms that are thought to be responsible for the phenomenon (e.g., the information processor). We show that this move is guided by a set of disciplinary assumptions about the relationship of explanation to causation, not by the demands of the phenomenon itself. We then identify two major problems that arise from this move to mechanism: 1) the problem of stagnation that occurs because little progress is made in verifying or falsifying any of the many competing mechanisms that have been suggested as explanations for altruism, and 2) the tendency of these mechanistic explanations to explain the phenomena that initiated the study in such a way that the altruism psychologists describe is something altogether different from what the altruist actually experiences. We conclude this section with a discussion of the paradox of a mechanistic approach to a study of altruism, which is that empirical psychological science often dismisses the empirical data of the altruists' experience in favor of metaphysical speculation about non-empirical psychological mechanisms.

Moving from Phenomenon to Mechanism

Psychological research, like most other forms of social scientific investigation, begins by taking up a common phenomenon or event of interest. A quick perusal of the main topics covered in any introductory psychology textbook reveals what sorts of phenomena prompt psychologists to pursue various programs of research. Sensation, perception, motivation, emotion, cognition, stress, memory, intelligence, consciousness, language, and so on are all phenomena people experience first and which become topics of study for psychologists second. Consider, for example, the phenomenon of human cognition. We first experience ourselves as thinking beings and we engage with other people who report that they too are thinking. In this process, we come to believe that this phenomenon of thinking is an important aspect of our humanity and that it is also involved in the occurrence of many other important psychological phenomena, such as acting and feeling. Given both its importance and apparent ubiquity, the question of the nature of cognition becomes a topic for psychologists to examine and explain.

Like cognition, altruism is a phenomenon we commonly experience or encounter in the course of our daily lives. We observe the phenomenon of selflessness in others, read about it in newspapers, hear about it in conversations, and may even experience it ourselves at times. For example, we may have seen television footage of an off-duty fireman plunging into the icy waters of the Potomac River to pull an exhausted plane crash survivor to shore, as another plane crash survivor, though badly injured and stranded on a wingtip in the water, keeps handing the helicopter safety harness to other passengers, until eventually he slips beneath the water and dies. We may watch video footage of a man jumping onto the subway tracks to protect and rescue a child he does not know from the dangers of an oncoming train. We might have read stories of people who gave away their last piece of bread or comforted others in Auschwitz (e.g., Frankl, 1992; Langbein, 2004).

Whatever the case, we are frequently struck by the poignancy of such events, as they seem to reveal something deeply significant about human nature – something vital to a more complete understanding of who we really are and of what we might actually be capable. We find ourselves wondering why it is these people did what they did, and we desire to understand the phenomenon and its meaning more fully. The psychologist, too, wonders about the phenomenon of altruism – and does so with a particular purpose and method in mind, and from within a particular conceptual and explanatory framework.

Psychologists often define their discipline as "the scientific study of behavior and mental processes" (Rathus, 2013, p. 4). As such, they are committed to a certain kind of explanation that uncovers the underlying psychological processes or mechanisms that account for the phenomena of interest. As Elster (1989) describes it, "To explain an event is to give an account of why it happened. Usually . . . this takes the form of citing an earlier event as the cause of the event we want to explain. . . . [But] to cite the cause is not enough: the causal mechanism must also be provided, or at least suggested" (p. 2-4). Consider again the example of cognition cited above. For most psychologists, a study of the phenomenon of thinking as it is experienced by the people doing the thinking is necessarily insufficient to provide a bona fide scientific psychological explanation of it. Rather, a causal mechanism of some sort must be suggested, a mechanism that can account for the phenomenon of thinking, both in terms of its content and its process.

The advent of the computer in the last century has suggested (by analogy) the mechanism of an information processor that could explain human cognition and has now become the focus of a great deal of psychological research and theorizing about cognition. Indeed, it has become common for cognitive psychologists to use computer parlance in their explanations of human thinking. For example, it is not unusual to hear the brain referred to as a "wet computer" (see, e.g., Cosmides and Tooby in press; Waller, 2007), complete with circuits, programming, data storage and other computer-derived features presumed to constitute its mechanisms and explain its operations (see, e.g., Coward, 2005; Legendy, 2009). This, in turn, is thought to provide a scientific explanation of the phenomenon of thought. For most cognitive psychologists, it is the mechanism of the information processing brain, and not the phenomenal experience of cognition itself, that is the conceptual key to a proper psychological explanation of cognition.

Similarly, psychological research on altruism typically proceeds from the assumption that there exists some underlying psychological mechanism that accounts for the apparent selfless behavior that people experience or observe in others. Simon (1990), for example, assumes that "human docility and bounded rationality" (p. 1665) are inherited, evolutionarily adaptive mechanisms that promote altruistic behaviors by rendering the altruist "unable to distinguish socially prescribed behavior that contributes to fitness from altruistic behavior" (p. 1667). In other words, docile people – those who tend to conform to social influence and have a limited rationality – are altruistic because they cannot independently evaluate the personal fitness consequences of their altruistic actions. They lack the full range of reason needed to understand the fitness losses that come from engaging in altruistic behaviors.

Along with evolution-based mechanisms like those proposed by Simon and other evolutionary thinkers (see, e.g., Sussman and Cloniger, 2011), neuroscience researchers have recently suggested certain neural mechanisms that may predict altruism (or at least "prosocial behavior"), mechanisms such as "activity in the posterior superior temporal cortex (pSTC), particularly in the right hemisphere" (Tankersley, Stowe, and Huettel, 2007, p. 1). Likewise, a number of researchers have proposed social mechanisms, such as reciprocity norms (e.g. Gouldner, A. W., 1960; Trivers, 1971; Triandis, 1978; McCullough, Kimeldorf, and Cohen, 2008; Nowak, 2006; Seinen and Schram, 2006), personality mechanisms and types of various sorts (Bierhoff, Klein, and

Kramp, 1991; Fagin-Jones and Midlarsky, 2007; Graziano, Habashi, Sheese, and Tobin, 2007; Oliner and Oliner, 1988; Penner, Fritzsche, Craiger, and Freifeld, 1995), and emotional mechanisms like negative state relief (Cialdini, Darby, and Vincent, 1973), responses to aversive arousal (Dovidio, Piliavin, Gaertner, Schroeder, and Clark, 1991; Piliavin, Dovidio, Gaertner, and Clark, 1981), and empathy (Batson, 1991, 2011). A prominent mechanism underlying many theories of altruism (or, at least, what is often termed "prosocial behavior") is paradoxically the mechanism of egoistic motivation (Cialdini, Baumann, and Kenrick, 1981; Maner, Luce, Neuberg, Cialdini, Brown, and Sagarin, 2005).

Traditionally, once an underlying mechanism is suggested, whatever it may happen to be, the final step in the research process is to generate hypotheses about the proposed mechanism that can be empirically tested and replicated. Thus, cognitive neuroscientists expend their research efforts in trying to identify the brain structures and pathways that are held to account for pattern recognition, language acquisition, memory, and so forth. As a result, many cognitive neuroscience researchers have come to believe that the brain is itself composed (like a computer) of many different modules or devices, each with specific functions that operate collaboratively to produce cognition, as well as feelings and behaviors (Callebaut and Rasskin-Gutman, 2005). Similarly, psychologists interested in the mechanisms that presumably explain altruistic behavior have focused their research on testing hypotheses concerning the genetic, neuronal, and/or psychological devices and processes held to be responsible for the actions of Irene and people like her (see, e.g., Oliner and Oliner, 1988; Smolenska and Reykowski, 1992; Sober and Wilson, 1998). The phenomenon that initiated the program of research in the first place has become secondary to the study of the psychological mechanisms that are thought to produce it and the actual experience of altruism itself has become, in certain fundamental ways, irrelevant.

Two Major Problems with Mechanism

Two important issues have arisen in the wake of this body of research on the mechanisms of altruism. First, as Batson and Powell (2003), Monroe (1996, 2002), Kohn (1990), Haski-Leventhal (2009), Kunz (1998) have pointed out, we really know little more about the nature and meaning of altruism than we did before this research was undertaken. As the evolutionary psychologist David Buss (1998) put it, altruism remains "puzzling and problematic" (p. 254). Second, the intense focus on mechanism has not so much explained the phenomenon of interest (i.e., altruism) as it has *explained it away*.

Stagnation

In regard to the first issue, there has been almost no progress in definitively determining what the psychological mechanisms are that might explain altruism. On the contrary, almost all of the mechanisms that have been proposed, including those that directly oppose one another, are still hanging around in the research literature, where they find both partisan support and critical challenge. Few, if any of the mechanisms that have been suggested, or the theoretical accounts in which such mechanisms play a central part, have ever been falsified. Indeed, it seems to be the case that radically different mechanistic accounts can be applied to the very same altruistic behaviors and still work equally well in explaining them, despite the often antithetical nature of their differences (see, e.g., Batson, 1991; Cialdini, Darby, and Vincent, 1973; Sober and Wilson, 1998).

To further illustrate this last point, we briefly review here one of the most significant debates in the history of psychological research on altruism. The controversy concerns two proposed and opposed mechanisms of altruism. On the one hand, Daniel Batson (1991) has proposed a psychological mechanism for altruistic behavior that is based on the prior presence of empathic concern. His empathy-altruism hypothesis suggests that when one person is confronted by another person in need of help the potential helper experiences a measure of personal distress. This distress motivates the person to find relief either by helping the sufferer or by escaping the situation. Both actions are motivated by an egoistic psychological mechanism. It is also possible, however, that the potential helper could empathize with the sufferer and then seeks to help the person, even when the potential helper could easily escape the situation instead. When this occurs Batson believes the helper is not egoistically motivated by their own distress but is altruistically motivated by a genuine desire to relieve the other person of their suffering. Thus, in this account, the mechanism of empathy is thought to bring about a genuinely selfless act. Over the years, Batson (2011) has conducted several creative empirical studies to support his empathy-altruism hypothesis.

On the other side of the persistent debate about the possibility of altruism, Robert Cialdini asserts that an egoistic mechanism is at play in all instances of helping behavior, even when that behavior happens to involve empathy. Cialdini and his colleagues have conducted studies very similar to those of

Batson, in which an experience of empathy is induced and helping behavior follows (see, e.g., Cialdini, Baumann, and Kenrick, 1981; Maner, et al., 2005). However, Cialdini and his colleagues claim that their research demonstrates that empathy can trigger egoistic needs for the social rewards that might come from helping others, as well as the fear of social punishments that might result from not helping another (Maner, et al., 2005). Following a lengthy rebuttal by Batson (1991), Cialdini, Brown, Lewis, Luce, and Neuberg (1997) conducted further research in which they argued that empathy creates in us a feeling of oneness whereby the self and other overlap, and it is this mechanism of oneness that ultimately accounts for helping behavior, rather than some genuinely altruistic motivation. In oneness the division between self and other is minimized to such a degree that the help given does not just provide a benefit to the person in need but also provides benefit to the self and, therefore, is not truly selfless.

Although this is a key debate in the history of altruism research, and one that remains unresolved, it is decreasingly discussed in the literature. Neither side is willing to concede to their opponents' theory, proposed mechanism, or contradictory research findings. While Batson does acknowledge that egoistic helping behaviors of the type Cialdini describes do exist, he nonetheless holds firmly to the position that there is a form of empathy that does not trigger either the pursuit of rewards and avoidance of punishment or a feeling of oneness that results in egoistically motivated helping. Rather, he believes in the possibility of an empathically induced altruism. Cialdini and his colleagues, in contrast, continue to claim that empathy is not sufficient to promote genuine altruism, but is rather just another (subtle) form of egoistic motivation for helping. Despite the fact that both researchers have devised several clever experiments, the debate appears to have reached an impasse, leaving the controversy surrounding egoistic and altruistic mechanisms stagnant.

If the application of ever more creative, nuanced, and sophisticated procedures, instruments, and analyses fails to resolve this type of debate and results in stagnation , there is good reason to ask whether the problem is really a methodological one at all. Even more directly, there is good reason to ask whether research pursuing some mechanism underlying altruism is even a good idea in the first place. In the case of the debate between Batson and Cialdini, for example, each of the mechanisms they propose continue to be discussed in the literature despite the fact that no new research has been conducted on either one in over a decade and the debate remains wholly unresolved. Similarly, all of the other mechanisms that have been proposed to explain altruism remain open as possibilities as well, although few of them have been subjected to any sustained empirical study over the last decade. The scientific study of altruism has stagnated with little or no agreement about the mechanisms presumed to underlie it. For psychologists, altruism is still just as "puzzling and problematic" (Buss, 1998, p. 254) today as it was 15 years ago, and as it was 15 years before then.

Explaining the Phenomenon Away

The second major problem with a move to mechanism is that in addition to generating very little traction for helping us to understand the mechanisms of altruism, psychologists' obsessive focus on suggesting and identifying underlying causal mechanisms has resulted in researchers and theoreticians moving ever father away from the actual phenomenon that prompted research interest in the first place. Where do we find Irene's experience in all of these mechanistic accounts? She did not describe her actions as being induced by empathy or a feeling of oneness, or reciprocity, mood maintenance, docility, or any other mechanism psychologists investigate. She, like most other helpers, stated simply that the people she encountered needed help and she helped them. How is it that this "simple" (Scott and Seglow, 2007, p. 1) experiential account given by the altruist herself is so far removed from the complicated and confusing theorizing on the psychological mechanisms thought to underlie the experience?

There are a number of reasons for this conceptual distance between the phenomenon and the mechanism, but we will discuss only one key reason here, which is that psychologists, in their commitment to a mechanistic explanation of the phenomenon inevitably move from the empirical to the metaphysical. That is, although the observations of the people involved in the experience (e.g., Irene and the Jews she rescued) and their recorded self-reports regarding their motives behind those experiences (e.g., "the Jews needed help so I helped them") are often available as empirical data, psychological researchers frequently choose to ignore those data in favor of studying something that is not directly observable and is often not reported by the people involved—a hypothesized mechanism. Why would adherents of a presumably empirical science, who try to avoid metaphysical speculation (Bordens and Abbott, 2005) by relying solely on the procedures of systematic empiricism (Stanovich, 2013), engage in such a seemingly paradoxical practice?

The noted philosopher and theologian Alvin Plantinga (2000) has taken up this very paradox, noting that Simon's mechanism of genetic docility and bounded rationality is supposed to explain the behavior of people like Mother Teresa, but can only do so by disregarding her and other people's observations of her actions, as well as the reasons she gave for carrying them out. Some psychologists justify this seeming dismissal of the empirical data attending the phenomenon by drawing a distinction between the content and the process of the phenomenon. Henry Newton Malony, for example, a noted psychologist who studies religious phenomena, speaks of his psychological study of the phenomenon of religious conversion this way: "I assume that religious conversions are different not in the psychological processes involved but in the content of the decision" (1998, para. 6). He illustrates his point by stating that, at the level of the psychological mechanisms responsible for conversion, which is his focus as a psychologist, "the decision of a Muslim to become a Moonie is no different than the decision to change from using an electric typewriter to a computer" (Malony, 1998, para. 5). The specific content involved in religious conversion here is completely irrelevant to her account of religious conversion. As a psychologist, Malony's concern is the general mechanism underlying all types of conversions, from the most mundane to the most transformative. Similarly, the content of Irene's particular experience of helping others, or Mother Teresa's, or that of anyone else is not directly important to the psychological processes of altruism, despite the clear empirical content of such experiences. Rather, what seems to be of most importance to contemporary psychological theorists is identifying the causal mechanisms undergirding all altruistic experiences. However, in the end, this seemingly scientific strategy does not "save the phenomena" (Duhem, 1985; van Frassen, 1991, 2002) as any genuinely scientific endeavor must.[2] Rather, it forces the psychologist into sacrificing the phenomenon as it is manifest in the empirical world of lived-experience in favor of the hypothetical operations of some inferred psychological mechanism or set of mechanisms presumed to be responsible for the existence of the phenomenon in the first place, and which, as such, are held to be more real and meaningful than the phenomenon itself.

This commitment to processes over content would make sense if the psychological mechanisms were actually empirically derived, or if they were

---

[2] One is reminded of Rolston's (1999) trenchant observation: "We often forget how everyday experience can demand certain things of the sciences. Science must save the phenomena, and if physics presents a theory of quarks that implies that I cannot wave to my friend, so much the worse for that theory. Astrophysics and microphysics must permit and deliver the world as something we can recognize at native range, reinterpret this range though they do at other scales. Likewise with biology, and if microbiology presents a theory of neurological synapses that implies that I cannot wave to my friend, so much the worse for that theory too" (p. xv).

otherwise clearly necessary to adequately understand the phenomenon at hand. If psychologists knew that these mechanisms did exist, and that persons were not only composed of but determined by them, then this focus on mechanism and causal explanation would be both reasonable and productive. However, as we have argued elsewhere (Gantt, Melling, and Reber, 2012), the mechanisms of psychological explanation are more metaphor than mechanism, more metaphysical presupposition than physical reality. They are not the sort of thing that does or could ever fall upon the retinae, or be placed in a shoebox where others might touch or measure them. They are speculative, inferential, and demanded by a particular explanatory strategy, and not because they are an empirical necessity. Further, the origins of contemporary psychological science's commitment to mechanistic explanation rests not so much on the data of actual empirical observation, but rather in a particular scientific worldview and its attendant philosophical presuppositions (see Bishop, 2007; Gantt, Melling, and Reber, 2012; Gantt and Williams, 2013). Indeed, this fascination with mechanism can justifiably be seen as a product of psychology's continuing "Newtonian legacy" (Gantt and Williams, 2013). Such presuppositions are not, however, metaphysically innocent. They profoundly inform mainstream psychological theorizing and research, and often in deeply problematic ways.

While it is beyond the scope of this chapter to critically evaluate the costs and benefits of psychology's adoption of the assumptions of natural science and its method generally, we do believe it is worthwhile to briefly examine the implications of this adoption for a psychological study of altruism specifically. We have already pointed out that one major implication of this mechanistic bias on altruism research is that many mechanisms have been postulated and almost none have been verified or falsified, including those that directly oppose each other. The result has been controversy followed by stagnation over the last decade. Because mechanisms have to be inferred and operationalized they cannot in principle be observed or experienced, and, thus, are seldom (if ever) reported by actual people experiencing altruistic intentions and engaging in altruistic actions. Thus, psychological researchers are always at least one vital step removed from the mechanism that is the focus of their research interest and efforts. Because mechanisms are not directly observable they are highly resilient to falsification using experimental methods, despite the often creative and nuanced manner in which such methods are increasingly applied. Variations in method, however, cannot solve the problems being discussed here because psychological mechanisms (as opposed to genuinely physical mechanisms) are metaphysical postulates and not empirical realities

(Gantt, Melling, and Reber, 2012). As a result, any psychological theorizing about altruism that is tied to conjecture about the existence and causal properties of one or another psychological mechanisms would seem to be doomed to remain entirely speculative in nature and, in the end, inescapably subject to the pressures of disciplinary fragmentation and theoretical partisanship.

In an effort to ameliorate this metaphysical and practical quagmire, a number of social and evolutionary psychologists have sought to replace the study of altruism, which implies unobservable intentions and motives of a self-sacrificing nature, with research into seemingly more accessible (i.e., directly measureable) helping or "prosocial" behaviors (Stürmer and Snyder, 2010). By emphasizing particular (presumably objective) behaviors rather than the subjective intentions of the helper these psychologists attempt to highlight the observable features of actions that in some way serve to benefit others. A majority of social psychology textbooks now use the more behavioral terminology of "pro-social behavior" or "helping behavior" as headings for that chapter in the text that would have previously been labeled "altruism" (see, e.g., Baumeister and Finkel, 2010). While this change in topic title may sound more empirical – and to have, thereby, sidestepped numerous sticky metaphysical issues – a quick perusal of the actual content of such chapters across these different texts shows that the content has not really changed at all. One still finds lists of various (fundamentally metaphysical) psychological mechanisms that are assumed to be the governing forces behind any particular helping behavior that happens to be observed. Each proposed mechanism is supported by its own set of studies in which the mechanism is never actually studied or empirically observed, but only operationalized and inferred. The window dressing may have changed somewhat but the product being sold is still very much the same.

From Mechanisms to Motives

Despite a disciplinary desire to make conceptual progress, most contemporary psychological research on altruism has not in fact moved very far beyond the metaphysical speculations of its less empirically inclined intellectual forbears of the late 19th and early 20th centuries. For example, Sigmund Freud argued that our conscious thoughts, behaviors, and feelings, no matter how noble in aspiration or sentiment, are in all cases betrayed by an unconscious intrapsychic mechanism that is rooted in fundamental egoism and which is the hidden but true source of our real motives (Freud, 1917; see also Wallach and Wallach, 1983). In this vein, Freud famously characterized parental love, often acknowledged to be a form of sustained altruism, as not really a matter of selfless love or caring for another at all, but rather an expression of an underlying and primary narcissism. "Parental love," he wrote, "which is so moving and at bottom so childish, is nothing but the parents' narcissism born again" (Freud, 1914, p. 91). Ultimately, such thinking, whether found in the psychoanalytic tradition of Freud or in contemporary psychological research on altruism, dictates that things are never really what they seem to be.

Although Freud's methods are often labeled unscientific, and his metaphysical constructs are now taken to be passé, his intellectual legacy of looking beyond or beneath the phenomena of lived-experience for other, presumably more basic, processes to explain such phenomena is still very much alive – as are all the attendant problems of such an approach to psychological understanding. As even the most cursory review of the mainstream psychological theories of altruism demonstrates, contemporary theories of altruism are rife with the presumption that any sufficiently scientific account of the phenomenon must invoke some manner of unconscious process, some hidden and subtle psychological machinery, capable of producing individual instances of altruistic behavior. Furthermore, such unconscious processes are typically thought to embody – by nature of their grounding in a fundamental egoism (Wallach and Wallach, 1983) – motivational forces whose aims are entirely antithetical to those of the particular altruistic behavior being studied. Thus, rather than seeing Irene's acts of giving aid to strangers in need as being produced by a basic desire to be of genuine service to those people in need, despite whatever possible costs or inconveniences such service might entail for her and her family, most contemporary theories of altruism demand that we see such behavior as the mechanical product of powerful hidden motives and unconscious forces that are firmly grounded in self-interest and hedonism. In short, when fully understood from a psychological point of view, Irene and other apparent altruists like her are really only self-deceived egoists.

But why is it that the great majority of contemporary psychological theorists follow Freud in assuming that egoism is a fundamental motivational force (Kohn, 1990; Wallach and Wallach, 1983), particularly in light of their typical rejection of his theoretical approach otherwise? Do the data demand an egoistic explanation, even when the behaviors appear to be altruistic, as in the case of Irene? Or, is it possible that egoism, like mechanism, is another pre-investigatory assumption of the psychological worldview? To answer these questions we must briefly examine the philosophical and cultural origins of the assumption of egoism in the next section, where we also consider the problematic implications this assumption of egoism creates for a genuinely scientific study of altruism.

The Problem of Egoism

Whether the motive to help is thought to arise out of some basic evolutionary dictate rooted in genetic selfishness (Dawkins, 1989), or from the inescapable desire to avoid negative feelings (Baumann, Cialdini, and Kenrick, 1981), or to generate positive feelings (Smith, Keating, and Stotland, 1989), the presumption of an inescapable selfishness reigns in psychological accounts of human behavior. Thus, whether there is some universal drive to optimize personal well-being (Snyder, Lopez, and Pedrotti, 2011, pp. 267-300), a causal impetus of feeling sufficient amounts of empathy (Batson, 1991), or some sophisticated unconscious calculation of costs and benefits aimed at maximizing instrumental outcomes (Hastie and Dawes, 2010), the possibility of genuinely acting out of a selfless concern for another is denied from the very outset by most contemporary theories of altruism, guided as they are by a prior philosophical commitment to egoism.

The philosophical doctrine of egoism – or, as it is often known, "psychological egoism" – has very long and distinguished history in the Western intellectual tradition, finding expression in the work of Ancient Greek philosophers such as Epicurus and Diogenes, as well as in more modern thinkers such as Hobbes, Hume, and Bentham (Rogers, 1997). Carrying the intellectual torch for their philosophical forebears, many theorists in psychology have been strong advocates for an egoistic perspective on the question of human nature. Not only Freud, but psychologists as diverse as B. F. Skinner, Carl Rogers, Albert Ellis, Robert Perloff, and David Buss have each offered their own accounts of human behavior that draw upon the assumption of psychological egoism (see Vitz, 1995; Wallach and Wallach, 1983). Indeed, echoing the Stoic philosopher Cato, who stated that "it is love of self which supplies the primary impulse to action" (cited in Rogers, 1997, p. 39), psychologist Martin Hoffman (2000) has claimed that contemporary research in psychology occurs in a context of "knowing full well that however much a person cares about others, when the chips are down, the individual thinks of himself first" (p. 1).

Intriguingly, Hoffman asserts here as fact what is in reality only an assumption – a widely shared and culturally dominant assumption, to be sure, but nonetheless an assumption. Indeed, it often seems as though most psychologists are not fully aware that egoism is neither an empirical fact of the world nor a logically necessary conclusion about the fundamental nature of human motivation. Rather it is nothing more than a philosophical proposition about the nature of human nature, and one that has a fairly specific point of origin in the history of ideas – as well as some cogent rebuttals (see, e.g., Adams, 2006; Algra, Barnes, Mansfeld, and Schofield, 1999; Flescher and Worthen, 2007; Rogers, 1997). It should come as no surprise, however, that psychologists often consider egoism to be a fact of nature, particularly given its pervasive manifestation in contemporary Western culture's commitment to consumerism, individualism, and a generally instrumental approach to interpersonal and social relationships (Bellah, Madsen, Sullivan, Swidler, and Tipton, 1985). After all, as human beings, psychologists are as much a product of the cultures they inhabit as they are contributors to it (Cushman, 1995). Thus, their questions, their methods of investigation, and their theoretical accounts of what they study both instantiate and reflect back their prior – and usually hidden – biases about how the world works and why. However, while all inquiry in psychology must begin from certain basic philosophical assumptions, it is possible to bring these assumptions to light and to critically examine them – both in terms of their general plausibility and their impact on the conceptual and empirical adequacy of the explanations they encourage (Slife, Reber, and Richardson, 2005; Slife and Williams, 1995).

As far as understanding altruism is concerned, it seems that theories grounded in the assumption of egoism present a two-fold problem. First, if psychologists reject an altruist's account of their conscious experience of helping, they must in its place then propose some *unconscious* forces and *hidden* drives in order to preserve egoism as an explanation for altruistic acts. This is, of course, problematic for any scientific endeavor that aspires to be genuinely empirical in nature because the empirical reality that psychological scientists face is that people frequently report acting out of a selfless concern for the welfare of others. Second, in assuming egoism (even in hidden or unintentional ways), the psychological theorist must replace the simple empirical account that is reported by altruists with the postulation of metaphysical entities or hypothetical processes (i.e., psychological mechanisms) that ultimately complicate rather than simplify explanation. This is clearly problematic for any science that values parsimony in its explanations (Bordens and Abbott, 2005).

Thus, psychologists who are confronted with accounts of altruism like that of Irene and others must decide whether to accept the accounts more or less at face-value and interrogate them at that empirical level or, at least to some extent, discount the validity of such accounts and resort to explanations grounded in the non-empirical and the unconscious (i.e., the metaphysical). The fact of the matter is that, for the most part, psychologists have chosen to deny the face-validity of such accounts and focus instead on unconscious psychological mechanisms. While this can be done, perhaps most cynically, by asserting that those reporting altruistic experiences are actually lying about their motivations – presumably out of a deeper desire to maximize personal advantage in some way – few psychologists have opted for this strategy. Rather, most researchers argue that although altruists usually provide an honest reporting of their experiences, they are nonetheless mistaken about the actual nature of those experiences because the real cause of their altruism lies in some unconscious egoistic processes – the nature and presence of which they are naturally and entirely unaware. Thus, rather than allowing investigation to remain at the level of the properly empirical and experiential, a hidden pre-investigatory philosophical bias towards egoism and the metaphysics of mechanisms paints the psychological theorist into a conceptual corner where all manner of hypothetical forces and unconscious processes must be postulated in order to account for altruistic actions and intentions. Not only does this fail to adequately "save the phenomena," as we noted above all legitimate scientific research must do, but it needlessly multiplies the number of hypothetical constructs and explanatory entities required for making sense of altruistic action and experience. Ultimately, parsimony is sacrificed on the altar of hidden philosophical presupposition right along with the conscious and meaningful experience of altruism shared by people like Irene and the people she rescued.

The Problem of Necessary Determinism

In addition to the effect that the pre-investigatory philosophical biases of mechanism and egoism have on the scientific and empirical quality of many explanations of altruism, these explanations are likewise shaped by another non-empirical, metaphysical presumption known as necessary determinism. Simply stated, necessary determinism is the notion that, given a particular set of antecedent causal conditions, a given subsequent event will occur as it must occur and could not have occurred otherwise. Although there are a variety of conceptions of determinism to be found in the literature of the social sciences, for the most part psychologists have embraced necessary determinism and the conception of causality that it entails (see Bishop, 2007; Martin, Sugarman, and Thompson, 2003). For example, in one widely-used text on research methods in psychology, Heiman (2001) identifies necessary determinism as a fundamental characteristic of the psychological explanation and defines it to mean that "behavior is *solely influenced* by natural causes and does not depend on an individual's choice or 'free will'" (p. 7; emphasis added). Further, he notes that psychological scientists:

> assume that you cannot freely choose to exhibit a particular personality or respond in a particular way in a given situation. The laws of behavior force you to have certain attributes and to behave in a certain way in a given situation. Anyone else in that situation will be similarly influenced, because that is how the laws of behavior operate. (Heiman, 2001, p. 7).

Thus, to conduct legitimate psychological inquiry at all means, at least according to this commonly accepted perspective, to employ fundamentally deterministic forms of explanation.

A classic illustration of this sort of thinking can also be found in Stanley Milgram's description of the general nature of social psychological inquiry:

> The social world does not impinge on us as a set of discrete variables, but as a vibrant, continuous stream of events whose constituent parts can be dissected only through analysis, and whose effects can be most compellingly demonstrated through the logic of experiments. Indeed, the creative claim of social psychology lies in its capacity to reconstruct varied types of social experience in an experimental format, *to clarify and make visible the operation of obscure social forces so that they may be explored in terms of the language of cause and effect*. (p. xix; emphasis added)

He further elaborated:

> The implicit model for experimental work is that of the person influenced by social forces while often believing in his or her own independence of them. It is thus a social psychology of the *reactive individual, the recipient of forces and pressures* emanating from outside oneself. (p. xix; emphasis added)

Here we see Milgram articulating a worldview in which persons are taken to be fundamentally passive respondents whose behavior is not only entirely a product of forces over which they have no control and in the origination of which they play no role, but who are also unaware of the actual origins of the forces commanding their behavior. The task of the psychological scientist, in such a scheme, is to employ sophisticated methods of observation, experimentation, and measurement in order to uncover the various forces and pressures governing individuals' behavior. In this perspective, the only relationship between the individual's behavior and the forces and pressures antecedent to it is one of necessary cause and effect. In the case of altruism, then, whether or not an individual acts in (or even intends to act in) an altruistic manner depends entirely on the particular causal forces that happen to be operating on that individual at a given moment, and not on any form of personal agency.[3]

Once again, however, the psychological scientist seeking to understand the nature and meaning of human behavior (e.g., altruism) in terms of necessary determinism is painted into a conceptual corner by what is in fact another pre-investigatory philosophical bias, and not an empirical fact. As Williams James noted almost 130 years ago in an essay entitled "The Dilemma of Determinism":

> The principle of causality . . . what is it but a postulate, an empty name covering simply a demand that the sequence of events shall some day manifest a deeper kind of belonging of one thing with another than the mere arbitrary juxtaposition which now phenomenally appears? It is as much an altar to an unknown god as the one that Saint Paul found at Athens. All our scientific and philosophic ideals are altars to unknown gods. Uniformity is as much so as free-will. If this be admitted, we can debate on even terms. But if anyone pretends that while freedom and variety are, in the first instance, subjective demands, necessity and uniformity are something altogether different, I do not see how we can debate at all" (1956, pp. 147-148)

In other words, determinism is neither the sort of thing that falls on the retinae as an empirical fact of nature, nor is it some sort of necessary truth required by reason and inescapably arrived at by logic. Rather, necessary determinism is a philosophical assumption, a metaphysical preference in explanation that is all-too-often held out as an inescapable feature of the world and, thus, something that any legitimate science of behavior must embrace or fail utterly at its most basic explanatory tasks. Such sentiment, even if it

---

[3] Indeed, the clear implication of pronouncements such as Heiman's is that the individual is incapable of exercising any personal agency in any situation because any such agency or "free will" quite simply does not exist.

happens to reflect a majority view in the social sciences, does not elevate determinism to the status of either unquestionable truth or indispensable element of genuine psychological investigation.

Whatever the ultimate epistemological status of necessary determinism and the causal world it entails, it seems clear that there are at least two significant problems with assuming necessary determinism in our psychological accounts of altruism (and, for that matter, any other meaningful human experience): (1) superfluous causal inference and (2) the denial of meaning. That is, because of a pervasive pre-investigatory philosophical bias towards seeing events in the world in terms of necessary and efficient causal relationships, psychologists studying altruism have consistently been obliged to offer up one or another sort of necessary and causal explanation for altruism in the absence of any compelling empirical reason for doing so. Consequently, it is often the case that in order to make deterministic explanations as consistent as possible, and to ensure acceptance by as wide an audience of fellow psychologists as possible, altruism researchers have been compelled to postulate all manner of hypothetical psychological mechanisms presumably capable of efficiently causing whatever altruistic behavior the researcher happens to be studying. As noted above, however, this strategy is one that inevitably leads to conceptual problems such as confusing metaphors with mechanisms and violating parsimony in scientific explanation via the superfluous proliferation of hypothetical constructs and unobservable processes.

The second, and perhaps more significant, problem with deterministic accounts of altruism concerns the way in which such accounts ultimately deny any meaningful substance to the interpersonal richness and moral vibrancy of altruism as it is experienced. That is, when an act of altruism is explained solely in terms of underlying necessary causal mechanisms, such an act is as it must be and cannot be otherwise because it is dictated by the antecedent conditions or forces responsible for its production. It is, thus, purely reflexive and mechanical in nature – like an eye blink in response to a puff of air or a knee jerk in response to the tap of a ballpeen hammer – and, therefore, has no intrinsic meaning or significance – moral or otherwise (Fuller, 1990; Slife and Williams, 1995). Acts of this sort simply are what they must be and are, thus, incapable of supporting any genuine claim to meaningfulness because meaning requires genuine possibility (see, e.g., Gantt and Burton, 2013; Guignon, 2002; James, 1897/1956; Martin and Sugarman, 1999; Martin, Sugarman, and Thompson, 2003; Slife and Williams, 1995; Williams, 2005). That is to say, for an event to be considered meaningful it must be genuinely possible for that event to have been otherwise than it was. Events that are necessarily determined are simply incapable of possessing any genuine meaning. For example, consider the tropisms of certain plants, the leaves of which slowly and mechanically bend and change position relative to the location of the sun as it moves across the sky. As a necessarily determined event this phenomenon is simply what it is, and, as such, is not inherently meaningful. Granted, someone who enjoys gardening and is, thus, very interested in plants and their "behavior" might find the movement personally meaningful for any number of practical, aesthetic, or even scientific reasons. However, that some movement can be meaningful to a particular subjectivity external to the organism actually doing the moving does not render the movement itself meaningful. In the case of human altruism, then, only if persons are in some fundamental sense genuinely capable of both intending and acting otherwise than they do (i.e., non-altruistically or otherwise) is it possible for any real meaning to be ascribed to their acts of altruism. Insofar as contemporary psychological theories of altruism of various stripes invoke necessary determinism to account for altruistic behavior, they deny the possibility that altruistic behavior or intention can be otherwise than it is, and, thus, deny that it possesses any inherent meaningfulness.

In this sense, then, despite the meaning her experiences during World War II may have had for her and for the Jews she rescued, as well as for those of us who read such stories, Irene's account is, at best, a fundamentally uninformative one. At worst, it is simply the report of an illusion. That is, if Irene's actions are simply the product of a unique set of natural causes that compelled her to action there is nothing meaningful or praiseworthy or genuinely humanitarian about what she did. Her behavior is fundamentally no different than that of a boulder rolling down a hill that has been dislodged from its resting place and moves according to the causal forces acting upon it. If the boulder happens to roll down the hill and crashes into a car full of bank robbers or murderers or rapists no one praises the boulder or gives it a medal for its actions, because the boulder is not responsible for its behavior. We may say it was at the right place at the right time and we may assign meaning to its action such as Karma or God's will, but none of that makes the boulder itself any more responsible for its actions or any more moral or good. It was simply the necessary effect of causes acting on it, which itself became the cause of another effect (hitting the car) in turn. No more, no less. Similarly, people may assign meaning to Irene's actions, but if the assumption of necessary determinism is true, then those meanings are misplaced because Irene is not responsible for her actions and, like a rolling boulder, she could not have done otherwise than what the causes acting upon her dictated.

However, as many scholars have shown, psychology's empirical realm of investigation is lived-experience and human meaning (see, e.g., Ashworth and Chung, 2010; Bishop, 2007; Brinkmann, 2011; Faulconer and Williams, 1990; Frankl, 1992; Fuller, 1990; Giorgi, 2001; Macmurray, 1961; Martin, Sugarman, and Thompson, 2003; Merleau-ponty, 1983; Slife and Williams, 1995). That is, meaning and the experience of meaning is central to what it means to be human. Meaning provides the fundamental horizontal context within which we act in the world, and within which are able to relate to one another in intentional and purposive ways. To be human is, therefore, at a most profound level, to be a meaning-making and meaning-navigating being inescapably situated at a nexus of historical, cultural, social, and moral relationships and possibilities. Meaning is the warp and woof of human existence and a fundamental empirical fact of that existence. Any psychology that aspires to be a science must, therefore, necessarily take into serious consideration this basic fact of human reality, and carefully assess any philosophical biases it might have that would require meaning in human action to be discounted or denied. Ultimately, any psychology science that privileges investigatory methods and theoretical formulations that deny meaning as central to what are in fact meaningful events is, whatever its pretensions might be, not in fact a genuinely empirical science at all.

Egoism, Rational Choice, and Determinism

Before concluding this analysis of determinism we feel it important to note that one possible objection to our analysis could be made by pointing out that a commitment to egoism in accounting for motivation does not necessarily commit one to deterministic forms of explanation. Rational Choice Theory (RCT), for example, is a popular approach to explanation that assumes egoism is a central and inescapable feature of all human action and intention (Gilboa, 2010; Hastie and Dawes, 2010; Lovett, 2006), but, as the name of the theory clearly suggests, individuals can choose from among alternative and competing courses of action in their pursuit to maximize self-benefit. It is hard to see how such a theory, or any of the many similar theories that have been derived from RCT, could possibly be legitimately criticized for assuming necessary determinism.

Despite such possible objections, however, we would contend that approaches such as RCT, even though they make much of rational deliberation and choice, are nonetheless undergirded with deterministic assumptions. For, while rational choice theorists argue that rational beings naturally weigh the various costs and benefits involved in aiding others who are in need and act on such deliberations, they also argue that whatever decisions the individual makes is necessarily determined by the fundamentally egoistic nature of human being and rationality. In other words, although a person may well be able to consider and choose from among a wide variety of possible costs and benefits to self in deciding whether or not to help another person in need, the one thing that the individual simply *cannot* choose to do is to *not* be driven by a fundamental egoistic concern for self. Any discussion of choice among alternatives (i.e., the various potential costs and benefits to self) present in such a conceptual and explanatory scheme is ultimately misleading since any choice that one might make concerning whether or not to go to the aid of another person has always already been dictated by the causal necessity of an inescapable egoism. Thus, whatever one might choose to do in a particular situation, the one thing that can never be chosen is to genuinely care for the welfare of another person more than for one's self.[4]

The situation here is metaphorically akin to finding oneself standing before an impressive and plentiful all-you-can-eat style buffet where a wide variety of enticing dinner choices have been laid out for your consideration, some of which are more preferable than others and some of which have higher potential costs than benefits, and vice versa. However, the rules of the establishment are such that while you are quite free to choose to eat whatever you happen to want, and in whatever amounts and for however long you wish, the one thing you simply are not allowed to choose is to not eat and retain your grip on rationality in so doing. In other words, to choose to not eat when confronted with both need (hunger) and opportunity (food) would be a completely irrational action. After all, according to RCT and its variants, no rational being could ever *rationally* choose to act irrationally, and, thus, there really is no sane choice but to eat. If the only alternatives to eating that are available are irrational ones, they are hardly genuine choices at all. Indeed, to draw the metaphor out a bit more, not only are the conditions of this particular buffet such that no one can choose to abstain from eating, or step out of line so

---

[4] Gantt (2000) has argued elsewhere that even if some formulation of RCT admitted the possibility of choosing to act in genuinely non-egoistic (i.e., altruistic) ways, given that rationality has been defined from the outset solely in terms of instrumental egoism, choosing to act in such a way could only be seen to be an irrational choice.

that others might dine instead, or even just give what one has to another with no thought of reciprocity, but it is not even possible for anyone to seriously (i.e., rationally) consider doing so. Ultimately, even though this necessary connection between egoism and determinism is seldom made clear in the psychological literature on altruism, it is nonetheless the case that the assumption of fundamental egoism necessarily precipitates a commitment to deterministic explanation.

A rational choice theorist might argue, and Irene might well agree, that she made a number of costs/benefit analyses in conducting her helping behaviors. Careful deliberation was required to determine the best methods of sneaking food and supplies out of the hotel where she worked. She had to consider how to avoid getting caught when she made her trips to the forest. She had to weigh the pros and cons of telling certain people what she was doing. Many rational and carefully thought out decisions were required of Irene concerning the timing and the methods of her rescuing efforts. But, as Monroe (1996) points out, there is a significant difference in the deliberations rescuers like Irene worked through concerning *how* they would help and the non-deliberated decision to help. The question of *why* Irene and other rescuers of Jews helped was never answered by rational choice. They just chose to help, and then they deliberated about how to best go about doing it after the choice had been made. After interviewing dozens of people like Irene, people who faced the prospect of almost certain death were their efforts to hide Jews discovered by the Nazis, Monroe (1996) notes: "Yes, rescuers knew the costs of their actions; there were far too many public executions and disappearances not to know the punishment for hiding Jews. The costs were simply never relevant to the rescuer's efforts to save lives" (p. 156). Indeed, as Irene herself noted: "I did not ask myself, Should I do this? But, How will I do this? " (Opdyke and Armstrong, 1999, p. 126). Fundamentally, altruism – particularly of the sort reported by Irene and so many others – is a matter of human intention and moral purpose, and not the simply byproduct of some rational calculus of self-interest or the mechanical playing out of hidden motives and deterministic forces.

We see this privileging of the *how* over the *why* in contemporary psychological research on altruism as a key conceptual confound. Questions of mechanisms and processes are *how* questions that may be appropriate to the decisions made about how to carry out the helping behavior a person is committed to. There may be cognitive decision trees, utilitarian calculations, and instrumental evaluations that are involved in the deliberations altruists engage in when they try to figure out how best to lend their aid to those in need. But the question of altruism is a *why* question, as is the question of egoism. These questions go to the heart of the person's intention. Why Irene chose to bundle up some food and throw it over the wall to the starving people on the other side is a very different question than the question of how she determined to get the food out of the hotel without detection. A proper study of altruism must examine Irene's intentions, not the mechanisms or processes that may be activated by those intentions.

CONCLUSION

When it comes to intentions, to the question of why altruists help others, there are, as we have already discussed, two choices researchers can make. They can investigate the descriptions of intentions given by the altruists themselves or they can rely on their own philosophical assumptions about human intentions. In this chapter we have examined several limitations of the latter approach. Research guided by the philosophical presuppositions of the researcher poses several challenges to the scientific credibility of the research, including problems of metaphysical speculation, stagnation and lack of falsification, a lack of parsimony, and a disregard for the empirically available phenomenon of interest. Along with these scientific problems there is a loss of the meaning and possibility that the experiences of altruism entail for those who experience them. The assumption of an egoistic determinism renders the phenomenon devoid of morality, humanity, and value. It is, at the end of the day, no more meaningful than a plant moving with the light of the sun or a boulder rolling down a hill. Any program of research that is guided more by the assumptions of the discipline than by the phenomenon of interest inevitably reveals more about the researchers' disciplinary and personal biases than it does about the phenomenon of altruism and the altruist's experience of it.

We suggest, as an alternative, an approach to the study of altruism that takes the empirical evidence of the altruist's experience seriously and investigates that experience fully as it is understood and articulated by the people involved. This does not imply that the researcher's presuppositions can be removed or completely controlled. The philosophy of science has shown that objectivity of that sort is impossible (Slife and Williams, 1995). Instead, researchers will have to take seriously the experience of the altruist and must identify and resolve points of contrast between that experience and their disciplinary and personal biases in a manner that maintains the integrity of the empirical data, which is the altruists' account of their behavior. In the case of our exemplar in this chapter, Irene, this means that the reasons she gives for her behavior must be respected and valued as data points that contribute to an understanding of the phenomenon of altruism and ought to be rigorously and systematically compared and contrasted with the data points of other accounts of altruism.

In short, in any legitimately empirical scientific approach to the question of human altruism, concerns for reliability and validity are very important, as is the demand for a parsimonious account, especially one that avoids unnecessary metaphysical speculation that forces the researcher to go beyond the people involved and their experiences in such a way as to render their experiences suspect or illusory. Thus, if we are to generate truly scientific accounts of human altruism, we must take seriously, as empirical data, altruists' reports of their experience, and do so without interpreting those reports through metaphysically speculative lens colored by unexamined philosophical assumptions. Furthermore, we must acknowledge the possibility that individuals are indeed capable of acting out of a real concern for the welfare of others, rather than demanding from the outset that all such acts be explained solely in terms of the mechanical operations of hidden egoistic motives. And, finally, if we are to take the meaningfulness of human experience seriously, as we must if our science is to be a truly empirical one, then we must admit that human actions (altruistic and otherwise) are fundamentally the province of human agents, living in a world of meaningful possibilities and who are, thus, genuinely capable of doing and being otherwise.

REFERENCES

Adams, R. (2006). *A theory of virtue: Excellence in being for the Good.* Oxford, UK: Oxford University Press.

Algra, K., Barnes, J., Mansfeld, J., and Schofield, M. (1999). *The Cambridge History of Hellenic Philosophy.* Cambridge, UK: Cambridge University Press.

Ashworth, P., and Chung, M. C. (Eds.) (2010). *Phenomenology and psychological science: Historical and philosophical perspectives.* New York, NY: Springer.

Batson, C. D. (1991). *The altruism question: Toward a social psychological answer.* Hillsdale, NJ: Erlbaum.

Batson, C. D. (2011). *Altruism in humans*. Oxford, UK: Oxford University Press.

Batson, C. D., and Powell, A. A. (2003). Altruism and prosocial behavior. In T. Millon and M. J. Lerner (Eds.), *The Handbook of Psychology*, vol. 5, (pp. 463-484). Hoboken, NJ: John Wiley and Sons.

Baumann, D. J., Cialdini, R. B., and Kenrick, D. T. (1981). Altruism as hedonism: Helping and self-gratification as equivalent responses. *Journal of Personality and Social Psychology, 40*(6), 1039-1046.

Baumeister, R. F., and Finkel, E. J. (Eds.) (2010). *Advanced social psychology*. New York, NY: Oxford University Press.

Bellah, R. N., Madsen, R., Sullivan, W. M., Swidler, A., and Tipton, S. M. (1985). *Habits of the heart: Individualism and commitment in American life*. Berkeley, CA: University of California Press.

Bierhoff, H. W., Klein, R., and Kramp, P. (1991). Evidence for the altruistic personality from data on accident research. *Journal of Personality, 59*, 263-280.

Bishop, R. C. (2007). *The philosophy of the social sciences*. London, UK: Continuum Publishing.

Bordens, K. S., and Abbott, B. A. (2005). *Research design and methods: A process approach* (6th ed.). Boston, MA: McGraw-Hill.

Brinkmann, S. (2011). *Psychology as a moral science: Perspectives on normativity*. New York, NY: Springer.

Buss, D. M. (1998). *Evolutionary psychology: The new science of mind*. Needham Heights, MA: Allyn and Bacon.

Callebaut, W., and Rasskin-Gutman, D. (Eds.) (2005). *Modularity: Understanding the development and evolution of natural complex systems*. Cambridge, MA: The MIT Press.

Cialdini, R. B., Baumann, D. J., and Kenrick, D. T. (1981). Insights from sadness: A three-step model of the development of altruism as hedonism. *Developmental Review, 1*, 207-223.

Cialdini, R. B., Brown, S. L., Lewis, B. P., Luce, C., and Neuberg, S. L. (1997). Reinterpreting the empathy-altruism relationship: When one into one equals oneness. *Journal of Personality and Social Psychology, 73*(3), 481-494.

Cialdini, R. B., Darby, B. L., and Vincent, J. E. (1973). Transgression and altruism: A case for hedonism. *Journal of Experimental Social Psychology, 9*, 502-516.

Coplan, A., and Goldie, P. (Eds.) (2011). *Empathy: Philosophical and psychological perspectives*. Oxford, UK: Oxford University Press.

Cosmides, L., and Tooby, J. (in press). *Universal minds: Explaining the new science of evolutionary psychology*. London, UK: Weidenfeld and Nicolson.

Coward, L. A. (2005). *A system architecture approach to the brain: From neurons to consciousness*. New York, NY: Nova Science Publishers, Inc.

Cushman, P. (1995). *Construcitng the self, constructing America: A cultural history of psychotherapy*. Reading, MA: Addison-Wesley Publishing.

Dawkins, R. (1989). *The selfish gene* (2nd ed.). Oxford, UK: Oxford University Press.

Dovidio, J. F., Piliavin, J. A., Gaertner, S. L., Schroeder, D. A., and Clark, R. D. (1991). The arousal: Cost-reward model and the process of intervention: A review of the evidence. In M. S. Clark (Ed.), *Prosocial behavior* (pp. 86-118). Newbury Park, CA: Sage.

Duhem, P. M. (1985). *To save the phenomena: An essay on the idea of physical theory from Plato to Galileo*. Chicago, IL: University of Chicago Press.

Fagin-Jones, S., and Midlarsky, E. (2007). Courageous altruism: Personal and situational correlates of rescue during the Holocaust. *Journal of Positive Psychology, 2,* 136-147.

Fancher, R. E. (1996). *Pioneers of psychology* (3rd ed.). New York, NY: W. W. Norton and Company.

Faulconer, J. E., and Williams, R. N. (Eds.) (1990). *Reconsidering psychology: Perspectives from Continental Philosophy*. Pittsburgh, PA: Duquesne University Press.

Flescher, A. M., and Worthen, D. L. (Eds.) (2007). *The altruistic species: Scientific, philosophical, and religious perspectives of human benevolence*. West Conshohocken, PA: Templeton Foundation Press.

Frankl, V. E. (1992). *Man's search for meaning: An introduction to logotherapy*. Boston, MA: Beacon Press.

Freud, S. (1914). On narcissism. In J. Strachey (Ed.), *The Standard Edition of the Complete Psychological Works of Sigmund Freud, Volume XIV (1914-1916): On the History of the Psycho-Analytic Movement, Papers on Metapsychology and Other Works* (pp. 67-102). London, UK: Hogarth Press.

Freud, S. 1917). General introduction to psychoanalysis. In J. Strachey (Ed.), *The Standard Edition of the Complete Psychological Works of Sigmund Freud, Volume XIV (1914-1916): On the History of the Psycho-Analytic Movement, Papers on Metapsychology and Other Works* (p. 356). London, UK: Hogarth Press.

Fuller, A. R. (1990). *Insight into value: An exploration of the premises of a phenomenological psychology*. Albany, NY: State University of New York Press.

Gantt, E. E. (2000). Cognitive psychology, rationality and the assumption of hedonism. *The General Psychologist, 35*(3), 82-87.

Gantt, E. E., and Burton, J. (2013). Egoism, altruism, and the ethics of personhood. *Journal of Humanistic Psychology*.

Gantt, E. E., Melling, B. S., and Reber, J. S. (2012). Mechanisms or metaphors: The emptiness of evolutionary psychological explanations. *Theory and Psychology, 22*(6), 823-841.

Gantt, E. E., and Reber, J. S. (1999). Sociobiological and social constructionist conceptions of altruism: A phenomenological critique. *Journal of Phenomenological Psychology, 30*(2), 14-38.

Gantt, E. E., and Williams, R. N. (2013). Psychology and the legacy of Newtonianism: Motivation, intentionality, and the ontological gap. *Journal of Theoretical and Philosophical Psychology*.

Gilboa, I. (2010). *Rational choice*. Cambridge, MA: The MIT Press.

Giorgi, A. (2001). The search for the Psyche: A human science perspective. In K. J. Schneider, J. F. T. Bugental, and J. f. Pierson (Eds.), *The handbook of humanistic psychology: Leading edges in theory, research, and practice* (pp. 53-64). Thousand Oaks, CA: Sage Publications.

Gouldner, A. W. (1960). The norm of reciprocity: A preliminary statement. *American Sociological Review, 25,* 161-178.

Graziano, W. G., Habashi, M. M., Sheese, B. E., and Tobin, R. M. (2007). Agreeableness, empathy, and helping: A person x situation perspective. *Journal of Personality and Social Psychology*, *93*, 583-599.

Haski-Leventhal, D. (2009). Altruism and volunteerism: The perceptions of altruism in four disciplines and their impact on the study of volunteerism. *Journal for the Theory of Social Behaviour, 39* (3), 271-299.

Hastie, R., and Dawes, R. M. (2010). *Rational choice in an uncertain world: The psychology of judgement and decision making*. Thousand Oaks, CA: Sage Publications.

Hoffman, M. L. (2000). *Empathy and moral development: Implications for caring and justice*. Cambridge, UK: Cambridge University Press.

James, W. (1956). The dilemma of determinism. In W. James, *The will to believe and other essays in popular philosophy* (pp. 145-183). New York, NY: Dover Publications. (Original work published 1884).

Kitzrow, M. A. (1999). An overview of current psychological theory and research on altruism and prosocial behavior. In R. G. Bringle and D. K.

Duffy (Eds.), *With service in mind: Concepts and models for service-learning in psychology* (pp. 19-34). Washington, DC: APA Press.

Kohn, A. (1990). *The brighter side of human nature: Altruism and empathy in everyday life*. New York: Basic Books.

Kunz, G. (1998). *The paradox of power and weakness: Levinas and an alternative paradigm for psychology*. Albany, NY: State University of New York Press.

Langbein, H. (2004). *People in Auschwitz* (H. Zohn, Trans.). Chapel Hill, NC: University of North Carolina Press. (Original work published 1995).

Legéndy, C. (2009). *Circuits in the brain: A model of shape processing in the primary visual cortex*. New York, NY: Springer Science.

Lovett, F. (2006). Rational choice theory and explanation. *Rationality and Society, 18*(2), 237-272.

Macmurray, J. (1961). *Persons in relation*. Amherst, NY: Humanity Books.

Malony, H. N. (1998). The psychology of religious conversion. Paper presented at the International Coalition for Religious Freedom Conference, Tokyo, Japan. Retrieved March 22, 2013 from http://www.religiousfreedom.com/index.php?option=com_contentandview=articleandid=338andItemid=18.

Maner, J. K., Luce, C. L., Neuberg, S. L., Cialdini, R. B., Brown, S., and Sagarin, B. J. (2005). The effects of perspective taking on helping: Still no evidence for altruism. *Personality and Social Psychology Bulletin, 28*, 1601-1610.

Martin, J., and Sugarman, J. (1999). *The psychology of human possibility and constraint*. Albany, NY: State University of New York Press.

Martin, J., Sugarman, J., and Thompson, J. (2003). *Psychology and the question of agency*. Albany, NY: State University of New York Pres.

McCullough, M. E., Kimeldorf, M. B., and Cohen, A. D. (2008). An adaptation for altruism? The social causes, social effects, and social evolution of gratitude. *Current Directions in Psychological Science, 17,* 281-285.

Merleau-ponty, M. (1983). *The structure of behavior*. Pittsburgh, PA: Duquesne University Press.

Monroe, K. R. (1994). A fat lady in a corset: Altruism and social theory. *American Journal of Political Science, 38* (4), 861-893.

Monroe, K. R. (1996). *The heart of altruism: Perceptions of a common humanity*. Princeton, NJ: Princeton University Press.

Monroe, K. R. (2002). Explicating altruism. In S. G. Post, L. G. Underwood, J. P. Schloss, and W. B. Hurlbut (Eds.), *Altruism and altruistic love:*

Science, philosophy, and religion in dialogue (pp. 106-122). Oxford, UK: Oxford University Press.

Monroe, K. R. (2004). *The hand of compassion: Portraits of moral choice during the Holocaust*. Princeton, NJ: Princeton University Press.

Nowak, M. (2006). Five rules for the evolution of cooperation. *Science, 314,* 1560-1563.

Oliner, S. P., and Oliner, P. M. (1988). *The altruistic personality: Rescuers of Jews in Nazi Europe*. New York: Free Press.

Opdyke, I. G., and Armstrong, J. (1999). *In my hands: Memories of a Holocaust rescuer*. New York, NY: Dell Laurel-Leaf.

Penner, L. A., Fritzsche, B. A., Craiger, J. P., and Freifeld, T. R. (1995). Measuring the prosocial personality. In J. Butcher and C. D. Spielberger (Eds.), *Advances in personality assessment* (pp. 147-163). Hillsdale, NJ: Erlbaum.

Piliavin, J. A., Dovidio, J. F., Gaertner, S. L., and Clark, R. D. (1981). *Emergency Intervention*. New York: Academic Press.

Post, S. G., Underwood, L. G., Schloss, J. P., and Hurlburt, W. B. (Eds.) (2002). *Altruism and altruistic love: Science, philosophy, and religion in dialogue*. New York, NY: Oxford University Press.Rathus, S. A. (2013). *Psychology: Concepts and connections, brief version*. Belmont, CA: Wadsworth Publishing.

Ricouer, P. (1970). *Freud and philosophy: An essay on interpretation* (D. Savage, Trans.). New Haven, CT: Yale University Press.

Rogers, K. (Ed.) (1997). *Self-interest: An anthology of philosophical perspectives*. New York, NY: Routledge.

Rolston, H. (1999). *Genes, Genesis, and God: Values and their origins in natural and human history*. Cambridge, UK: Cambridge University Press.

Rushton, J. P., and Sorrentino, R. M. (Eds.) (1981). *Altruism and helping behavior: Perspectives from developmental, personality, and social psychology*. Hillsdale, NJ: Erlbaum.

Schroeder, D. A., Penner, L. A., Dovidio, J. F., and Piliavin, J. A. (1995). *The psychology of helping and altruism*. New York: McGraw-Hill.

Scott, N., and Seglow, J. (2007). *Altruism*. New York, NY: Open University Press.

Seinen, I., and Schram, A. (2006). Social status and group norms: Indirect reciprocity in a repeated helping experiment. *European Economic Review, 50,* 581-602.

Shaver, R. (1999). *Rational egoism: A selective and critical history*. Cambridge, UK: Cambridge University Press.

Simon, H. A. (1990). A mechanism for social selection and successful altruism. *Science,* 250(4988), 1665-1668.

Slife, B. D., Reber, J. S., and Richardson, F. C. (2005). *Critical thinking about psychology: Hidden assumptions and plausible alternatives.* Washington, DC: APA Press.

Slife, B. D., and Williams, R. N. (1995). *What's behind the research? Discovering hidden assumptions in the behavioral sciences.* Thousand Oaks, CA: Sage Publications.

Smith, K. D., Keating, J. P., and Stotland, E. (1989). Altruism revisited: The effect of denying feedback on a victim's status to empathic witnesses. *Journal of Personality and Social Psychology,* 57(4), 641-650.

Smolenska, M. Z., and Reykowski, J. (1992). Motivations of people who helped Jews survive the Nazi occupation. In P. M. Oliner, S. P. Oliner, L. Baron, L. A. Blum, D. L. Krebs, and M. Z. Smolenska (Eds.), *Embracing the Other: Philosophical, psychological, and historical perspectives on altruism* (pp. 213-225). New York, NY: New York University Press.

Snyder, C. R., Lopz, S. J., and Pedrotti, J. T. (2011). *Positive psychology: The scientific and practical explorations of human stengths.* Thousand Oaks, CA: Sage Publications.

Sober, E., and Wilson, D. S. (1998). *Unto others: The evolution and psychology of unselfish behavior.* Cambridge, MA: Harvard University Press.

Stanovich, K. E. (2013). *How to think straight about psychology* (10th ed.). Boston, MA: Pearson.

Stürmer, S., and Snyder, M. (Eds.) (2010). *The psychology of prosocial behavior.* Malden, MA: Wiley-Blackwell.

Sussman, R. W., and Cloniger, C. R. (Eds.) (2011). *Origins of altruism and cooperation.* New York, NY: Springer.

Triandis, H. C. (1978). Some universals of social behavior. *Personality and Social Psychology Bulletin,* 4, 1-6.

Trivers, R. L. (1971). The evolution of reciprocal altruism. *Quarterly Review of Biology,* 46, 35-57.

van Frassen, B. (1991). To save the phenomena. In R. Boyd, P. Gasper, and J. D. Trout (Eds.), *The philosophy of science* (pp. 187-194). Cambridge, MA: The MIT Press.

van Frassen, B. (2002). *The empirical stance.* New Haven, CT: Yale University Press.

Vitz, P. (1994). *Psychology as religion: The cult of self-worship* (2nd ed.). Carlisle, UK: The Paternoster Press.

Wallach, M. A., and Wallach, L. (1983). *Psychology's sanction for selfishness: The error of egoism in theory and therapy*. San Francisco, CA: W. H. Freeman and Company.

Waller, J. (2007). *Becoming evil: How ordinary people commit genocide and mass killing* (2nd ed.). Oxford, UK: Oxford University Press.

Westfall, R. S. (1977). *The construction of modern science: Mechanisms and mechanics*. Cambridge, UK: Cambridge University Press.

In: Psychology of Altruism   ISBN: 978-1-62808-152-7
Editor: Helena Koppel   © 2013 Nova Science Publishers, Inc.

Chapter 2

THE EVOLUTION OF FEELING

Michael Slote

Philosophy Department, the University of Miami, Florida, US

ABSTRACT

There has been a great deal of interest lately in "evolutionary psychology" as it relates to human moral psychology and other aspects of human thought and culture. The present chapter considers how morality seen as depending on altruism and on empathy as essential to such altruism might conceivably have evolved. This will require some evolutionary speculation, but also a great deal of conceptual analysis. We have to consider how empathy helps to make altruism possible, but also how evolution could have moved toward empathic creatures via a series of steps each of which had survival value. It will be argued, among other things, that an instinct for proximity helps produce creatures who are open to mutual empathic influence, and also that instincts of imitation (loosely understood) serve to bridge the gap between proximity (flocking, herding) and full-blown empathy. The role of mirror neurons in all this will be considered, as will the usefulness of mammalian mothering as a basis for a kind of generalized human sympathy that has evolutionary survival value.

INTRODUCTION

I am not a biologist. But a philosopher can learn from work in evolutionary biology and can conceptually/theoretically organize scientific findings in ways that at the very least are useful to the purposes of philosophy. Philosophers and ethicists in particular are now interested in issues about evolution that bear on the nature of morality and much of the work that philosophers have done in this area falls under the heading of evolutionary psychology (a less socially and intellectually controversial successor to the earlier field of research known as sociobiology). And what I do here will count as evolutionary psychology. But of course evolutionary psychology has to pick its targets, has to choose *what* it seeks to explain in evolutionary terms, and as a philosopher and ethicist my interest is in understanding or speculating about how we might profitably understand the evolution of human morality.

Now some people working on this topic are motivated by a desire to consider whether or how morality, as explainable in evolutionary terms, could really be as objective or objectively valid as we pre-philosophically think it is and as most ethicists over the millennia have considered it to be. But although that is a highly interesting topic and one I hope eventually to discuss at some length, it won't be the focus of the present discussion. Rather, I will concentrate on questions about how morality *understood in a certain way* might have evolved. In the field of moral education, philosophers, educationists, and psychologists typically presuppose ideas about what morality is or involves as its content and then discuss how parents, teachers, and others can educate children so that they exemplify or conform to morality conceived in those terms. And I believe that any useful evolutionary account of or speculation about morality needs to assume (or argue for) a view of what the "target" of evolutionary-psychological explanation actually is. At any rate, that is what I shall do here. So I want to begin by discussing how I am understanding morality, before I then go on to speculate about how morality might have evolutionarily developed.

1. WHAT IS MORALITY?

I am going to make, and make some initial efforts to justify, various assumptions about the nature of morality that are at least somewhat controversial in the field of philosophy. The Kantian ethical tradition is very strong nowadays and has wielded a great deal of influence within ethics during the past several decades (largely due to the personal/intellectual influence of John Rawls). And paradigmatic or ideal-typic Kantianism sees morality as based on or in (practical) reason and respect for the rules, principles, ideals that can be justified through reason. This means that the sheer desire to help others is not a primary aspect of morality. In other words, Kantians don't regard compassion, benevolence, sympathy, caring, and altruistic motivation in general as central or foundational to morality—morality is seen, rather, as involving a respect for reason, for moral duty seen as deriving from reason, and for other people seen as exemplifying the capacity for rational moral conscientiousness or dutifulness.

But this Kantian view is not commonsensical. Common sense and ordinary moral intuition see a moral/rational conscientiousness that is devoid of human/humane emotional involvement with and concern for others as morally questionable or worse, and I propose to go along with common sense in this chapter. Kantians may try to offer an evolutionary explanation of morality seen as independent of sympathy/compassion (I understand that Christine Korsgaard is working on such a project), but I think it accords better with our ordinary moral intuitions and with what previous evolutionary psychologists have said about the origins of morality, if we focus on altruism, sympathy, and similar moral-psychological human phenomena as our target of evolutionary explanation.

Now philosophical readers might at this point say that this is to give the game away as far as the issue of the objectivity of morality is concerned. For the idea that morality is principally a matter of benevolence, sympathy, and altruism comes from the moral sentimentalists, and especially Hume, and that tradition notoriously argues against seeing morality as being as objective as Kantians and other rationalists conceive it to be. However, I wrote a whole book, *Moral Sentimentalism* (Slote, 2010) defending sentimentalism from this rationalist charge. It explains why I think sentimentally-understood morality needn't be seen as undercutting moral objectivity and can actually help us explain why and how morality "succeeds" in being objective, in offering us objective moral truths. But I'm not going to repeat those arguments here. I am just going to assume that morality centrally involves altruism and altruistic motivations/attitudes like compassion, kindness, sympathy for others, and benevolence.

And I shall leave aside issues of deontology and justice. I believe and *Moral Sentimentalism* sought to show that these topics can be fully compassed in sentimental terms, but there is no need to assume or try to argue for that conclusion here. It will be enough if we can assume that compassion, sympathy, and the like are central to morality, the moral life; and a wide range of non-Kantian ethicists are and have been willing to grant this point--even when they have felt that justice/deontology remains an important independent aspect of morality (that might require its own kind of evolutionary explanation). So I see my task here as trying to better understand how altruism, sympathy, benevolence can plausibly be thought to have evolved.

2. THE PSYCHOLOGY OF ALTRUISM

In order to be able fully and relevantly to speculate about the evolutionary origins of morality, we need some further assumptions. I have just said a bit about what I take morality to be, and I concluded (at least for the purposes of this chapter) that morality as human beings exemplify it involves altruistic/sympathetic motivation(s). But I think we need to say and speculate just a bit about the ontogenesis of such motivation(s) if we want to say something relevant about phylogenesis. We need to say something about how sympathy for or benevolence toward others develops in individual children *in order to pinpoint the human psychological mechanisms that need to be accounted for in evolutionary terms*. Now there has recently been a good deal of psychological literature questioning the idea that human beings ever are genuinely altruistic toward others (Batson, 2011). Many of the arguments against altruism and in favor of psychological egoism seem to me to involve conceptual confusions, and I have elsewhere spelled out this reaction to the recent literature at considerable length (Slote, forthcoming). But I am here just going to assume that we are capable of altruistic motivation and will merely speculate about how such motivation can ontogenetically come about or fail to come about in human beings, especially human children. And my discussion of this topic will not be lengthy because I want to get on with the main topic of this chapter, the evolution of human morality understood as centrally involving altruism.

If we are going to understand the origins and development of benign human motivations and emotions like benevolence and sympathy, I think we first need to say some more about empathy. I indicated above that like many others working on issues of moral development/education, I believe empathy is a precondition of moral altruism and helps to sustain and strengthen it. But we have to be careful here. The term "empathy" has (at least) two uses among psychologists of moral development. According to one of those uses, we have empathy with another when we put ourselves in their place or in their shoes or their heads, and this sort of empathy is appropriately called projective empathy. But when Bill Clinton said he felt other people's pain, he was talking about another kind of empathy, a kind that conveys feeling or emotion from one person to another. Projecting oneself into another is typically deliberate and active, whereas when we feel another's pain or joy, this typically doesn't occur by or through any intention or choice of our own. It tends to occur automatically and involuntarily by a kind of osmosis, and it is less a matter of being active than of being receptive to the pain or joy or feelings of others. This latter kind of empathy, the kind Clinton was indirectly referring to, can conveniently be called "associative empathy"--though one should note that such processes of feeling transfer often depend on the cognitive capacities of the person who feels what another feels and are thus not always a matter of pure feeling.

Now I mention this distinction in empathy because it is crucial to clarifying what I said earlier about the causal relation between empathy and sympathy/benevolence. Psychopaths are very capable of getting into other people's heads for their own manipulative or malign purposes, but they aren't capable of associative empathy: they don't feel other people's sorrow, for example, but instead can feel joy at someone else's sorrow. And it is the fact that psychopaths are capable neither of associative empathy nor of altruistic motivation, e. g., genuine sympathy for others, that gives some initial plausibility to the idea that empathy in the fullest sense, empathy as involving a capacity for feeling what others feel, is required for and helps to sustain altruistic/sympathetic motivation and emotion. So when I now speak of empathy, I will mainly have associative empathy in mind, and the question we need to consider, therefore, is how associative empathy can ground sympathy/benevolence in humans. (If empathy is, for example, feeling another's pain, then sympathy means being sorry that they are in pain and wanting their pain to cease or diminish.)

Now there is evidence that we are capable of empathy even as babies. Babies can be affected by the moods of those around them (neonates in the hospital can start crying if one particular neonate begins to cry). This is much more primitive than the associative empathy that occurs later on and that depends to some extent on the concepts we have and what we know about the world (one can't feel empathy for a character in fiction without having considerable conceptual resources). But primitive or not, the kind of associative empathy that is available to babies and toddlers is, in my opinion, the original and main basis for human sympathy and altruism *when they occur*.

I add this last phrase because, as I suggested above, there are some humans, sociopaths or psychopaths (they are usually not distinguished), who lack sympathy for and benevolence toward others, who never act altruistically. And according to many psychological accounts, the processes that turn someone into a psychopath begin at a very young age.

Some accounts of psychopathy attribute it to genetic neurological defects and/or to events that do damage to brain structures/functioning (Mealey, 1995). But there is a widespread belief among clinical psychologists that this isn't, that this can't be, the whole story. Rather, it is held that parental neglect or abuse can help make a child into a psychopath and that this psychological damage can and typically does occur in the first two or three years of life (Bowlby, 1952). Almost no one thinks psychopaths can be cured, but to understand how such severe and long-lasting psychological damage can occur, we need to speak first about the more normal case, the case where parental treatment is good enough so that the capacity for altruism that the psychopath lacks takes hold in a child who has been treated lovingly by his or her parents. How does parental love lead a child with an inborn capacity for empathy to acquire the kind of basic sympathy for others that is pretty clearly a pre-condition and launching pad for (eventual) altruistic behavior? (I will briefly talk more about how psychopathy develops after dealing with this first question.)

So we begin with a young child, a baby, who has the capacity for empathy with the moods, feelings, and (eventually) attitudes of those around them, and I won't be more specific about how young a child or baby we are talking about here. Let's suppose too that the baby is loved by its parents: both its parents, of course, but since mothers have played the most important role in childcare and continue to do so, let us focus on what the mother does and is. (We will see shortly that evolutionary explanations will accord a certain primacy to the care mothers rather than fathers standardly give to babies.) The mother loves her baby and takes loving care of him or her even if she is sometimes frustrated and irritated about the demands of motherhood and mothering. But given what we said about babies just above, doesn't that mean that the baby or young child will pick up on how the mother feels about them? And given that this occurs via empathy, won't it mean that the baby osmotically takes in the mother's loving attitude? (The same thing, often less intensely, can happen between babies and their fathers.)

Now think what this means. When I receptively or osmotically take in another's pain, I feel something like what they are feeling. (Research on mirror neurons indicates that when this happens we feel, we take in, the emotions of

the person in pain more readily than the specific quality of their pain as a pain-
-e. g., it's sharpness or throbbingness.) So I believe we should say that a child
or baby who is loved takes in the emotional quality of that love in the sense of
feeling something like what the mother (or father) feels. And this feeling, this
loving attitude on the part of the mother (or parent) has two sides to it. The
mother feels love for her baby, for that particular offspring, and if the baby
takes that in, it will (arguably) feel a kind of love for itself, a primitive kind of
self-love. But the mother is also feeling and showing sympathy, something
that, given common usage, one feels toward others and not toward oneself. So
if the baby takes in the mother's sympathy as the state of sympathy it is, the
child will feel a kind of primitive "sympathy for the other." If the mother is
capable of sympathy for others and displays that capacity in actual sympathy
for the child, then some of this will, so to speak, rub off on the child. The child
will take in sympathetic feeling from its mother and have such feeling--and the
capacity for such feeling--within it.

Later forms of moral education can make use of someone's empathic
capacities to enhance, strengthen, and direct such sympathetic feeling
(Hoffman, 2000, Slote, 2010), but my hypothesis is that all these later
developments depend on the original taking in of (the capacity for) sympathy
from loving parents or a mother via associative empathic osmosis. And what
may typically or frequently happen with children who eventually become
sociopaths is that there was no maternal or parental love for them to take in.
But there is another element in this equation that needs to be mentioned: the
need for love. Children, even babies, have such a need, and among other
things this means that if a child's physical needs and comfort are attended to,
but the child isn't treated lovingly, they will feel that lack sorely. There is a
good deal of evidence that unloved children will tend to act out even if their
material needs are tended to. But children will certainly have a strong reaction
if even their physical needs aren't met and are likely to have an even stronger
reaction if they are physically or sexually abused.

Many psychopaths come from family backgrounds where they were
emotionally neglected or actually abused, and if we assume that they or many
of them were originally capable of associative empathy, one has to try to
explain how it is that that capacity is destroyed in those who eventually are
labeled as psychopaths. But an explanation is forthcoming if we assume a need
for love on the part of the babies who become adult psychopaths. If their
parents lack love for them, the empathic baby will register that fact, that
unfortunate reality; and the understandable reaction, when such a basic need is
felt not to be being met, is anger or rage. And we know from the literature on

empathy and present-day common sense also tells us that rage at or anger with someone tends to block or undercut empathy with that person. (Consider the normal reaction if a person one has liked and associated with does something terrible to one or to one's family.) If the need for love is basic and it is denied, a child is likely to feel great and persisting anger with their parents and with the world in general, and this precisely undercuts or can undercut the possibility of feeling empathic concern or sympathy for other people. So I am saying that when psychopathy results from parental mistreatment, it basically results from anger, even hatred, at having a basic desire frustrated. And that anger, if felt deeply and irrecusably, undercuts the capacity for empathy with others. Such a child or eventual adult didn't have parental or mother love that they could take in as a form of generalized sympathy with or for others, but instead were deprived of needed love in a way that made them permanently angry and incapable of either empathy or sympathy with others. But having said as much, we should proceed to the main topic of the paper. We have said enough about the ontogenesis of sympathy and altruism and about their centrality to morality so that we have a very appropriate, visible and, if I may say, rich target for evolutionary-psychological explanation. So let's proceed to the explanation.

3. THE EVOLUTION OF ALTRUISM

It is now time to talk about how our morality could have evolved through evolutionary steps each of which had survival value, but I am not going to try to recapitulate the entire history of life on Earth. We need to start somewhere, and I propose that we start with land animals that have evolved out of sea creatures and in particular with reptiles (though I will also have something to say about fish). The principal question will be how we could get from reptiles to humans with their undoubtedly imperfect moral capacities and habits. But, of course, for that to have happened, we first need the emergence of mammals from reptiles, and let me say something about that process that we can then make further use of or at least presuppose when we focus on the evolutionary elements of morality in particular.

Reptiles and (placental) mammals differ in many ways but two of those ways are especially salient for most of us. Reptiles are cold-blooded (poikilotherms) whereas mammals are warm-blooded (homeotherms); reptiles reproduce via eggs whereas mammals bear their young alive and feed them milk from their own bodies. So part of the explanation of human evolution and of the evolution of human morality has to speak to the advantages of warm blood and of breast-feeding, and evolutionary biology as it stands has a good deal to say on these topics. Warm blood allows land creatures greater flexibility in regard to where they live and the kinds of things they can do (I am being deliberately vague here), and lactation and breast feeding allow a mammalian mother to internally pre-prepare the food its young offspring need in order to thrive in a way that isn't possible when eggs are hatched separately from a mother. And even birds, who macerate worms or grubs in their mouths before giving them to their babies, can't control the nutrient and healthful aspects of what they feed their offspring to the extent that breastfeeding makes possible. What I am saying here should be familiar to most of you and not just to the biologists or medical doctors among you, and I shall presuppose it in my (personal) speculations about the evolutionary steps from reptiles to moral creatures like ourselves. (I will later say something about how apes and other creatures that are sometimes said to possess forms of morality fit into this picture.)

I propose to break down this issue of evolutionary steps into two distinct but related questions. The picture offered above of how, ontogenetically, a baby or young child comes to be sympathetic with others (which is, I contend, the first and most essential step of human moral development) describes a mother--or father, but in the evolutionary history of humans it was women who did most of the work of childrearing--who cares for her child in a loving manner and a child whose inborn capacity for empathy causes it to take in that mother's love/sympathy as sympathetic feeling of its own. So our task here may be somewhat simplified and clarified if we to some extent focus separately on how such a mother and how such a child could have been selected for. And I think we should begin with the mothers.

Maternal instinct is not the exclusive possession of mammals. Many birds show maternal instincts of caring for their young, and so do some reptiles. Crocodile mothers, for example, take care of their young for several weeks after they have hatched, defending them against predators and providing them with water during that period. And rattlesnakes in the United States also protect their young rather than abandoning them at hatching (Milius, 2004). Clearly maternal solicitude has evolutionary advantages whether it is in reptiles, in birds, or in mammals. But the solicitude of human mothers is of a very special sort. Neither reptiles nor birds are thought to be capable of empathy, and empathy allows a human mother to be in touch with and knowledgeable about how a baby is reacting to what she is doing to or with it-- in a way or to a degree that doesn't seem possible for birds or reptiles, and such knowledgeability has evolutionary advantages in terms of the thriving or even the survival of offspring. So the advantages of human mothering rest on empathy (among other things), and I haven't yet said anything about how empathy might have evolved. To be sure, empathy gives us an advantage over reptiles, but the phylogenetic evolutionary process of "producing" empathy doesn't just leap from non-empathic reptiles and birds to empathic humans. For one thing, humans develop out of a mammalian family tree, and some of the animal families on that tree may themselves lack the capacity for empathy.

Those who study empathy often say that empathy isn't limited to primates: that empathy can be found in dolphins, elephants, and social mammalian carnivores like wolves. But things become less clear with regard to other mammalian species and families. There is anecdotal evidence that empathy exists in the cat family, but I have never read of anyone claiming that horses or sheep have empathy. So for present purposes, let's assume that not all mammals have empathy. And if that is the case, then we should expect that those mammals that are capable of empathy (and there is no evidence of empathy in anything other than mammals) developed from mammals who didn't possess empathy. But how did this occur?

Fortunately, we can bring in mirror neurons to help us here. Some researchers claim (tentatively) that mirror neurons operate in all mammals and in birds, but not in cold-blooded animals (*European Science Foundation News*, 2008). And if that is correct, then we are dealing with three basic levels here: animals (like reptiles or fish) that lack mirror neurons, animals that have them but lack empathy, and animals whose mirror neuron functioning serves as a basis for empathy. And we need to consider not only how mirror neurons can represent an evolutionary advantage even in the absence of empathy, but also how empathy represents an advantage for creatures that already have mirror neurons.

I have been saying that humans are capable of empathy even early in their lives, so let's consider what sort of advantage this represents. We earlier mentioned the cognitive advantage a mother has when she can empathize with how her child is feeling or reacting, but surely the same point holds when we focus on the child or baby who has such a mother (or any sort of mother). Empathy will allow the baby or young child to be sensitive to their mother's (or father's) moods and emotions, and this has survival value. A child who knows, for example, when its parents are angry with it will be more able to avoid or defuse such situations than a child who cannot do this, and, as I say, this ability is obviously useful to children. And then there is the point stressed earlier in this chapter that a baby or child who is empathically sensitive will be able to osmotically register maternal sympathy as its own sympathetic state, and recent work in evolutionary psychology suggests that animals who learn sympathy in this way have (individually and together) evolutionary advantages over animals who don't learn to be sympathetic toward or with one another (Joyce, 2006). So empathy represents an advantage from the standpoint both of mothers and of their offspring.

But we then have to ask what kind of advantage mirror neuron functioning represents in the absence of the kind of higher or more complex mirror neuron functioning that empathic processes require. And in order to answer this question we will have to go back again to reptiles in our evolutionary thinking. Aside from the relation to empathy, the most striking thing about mirror neuron functioning is its role in imitation. If an animal possessing mirror neurons sees a conspecific perform some obvious visible action, the mirror neurons in its brain will mirror what is happening in the brain of the animals performing the action. And research on mirror neurons indicates that such a process of neurological mirroring typically occurs when animals, including human babies and adults, imitate or mimic one another. However, the scientists who study imitation often insist on distinguishing true imitation from forms of behavior that most people would call imitation, but which differ in important ways from the phenomenon or phenomena for which the scientists in question want to reserve the term "imitation" (Byrne, 2002). But rather, in this limited space, attempt to enter into this distinction-making, let me just use the term imitation in a colloquial way. In other words, I propose to treat as imitation anything to which we would normally apply the label "imitation."

Now the evolutionary advantage of imitation even in the absence of empathy lies in its usefulness to social groups and to the individuals in them (Rochat, 2002). To imitate a conspecific (especially an older conspecific) is to learn to do something that the older and presumably more experienced older conspecific has found helpful (or at least not harmful), so the habit or instinct of imitation allows for a useful social transmission of practical knowledge, even when we is being copied or imitated is just behavior. And there is also reason to think that apart from its role in the transmission of practical knowledge or information, imitation operates as a kind of invitation to further social connection between the animals imitated and the animal that imitates. And if imitation helps to increase social connection or sociability, that too can have positive benefits both at the level of individuals and at the level of groups. But empathy is a kind of copying or imitating of inner emotional or attitudinal states, and this more sophisticated or internally-directed kind of imitation has the advantage, as I said above, of allowing for the development of moral motivation in a way that sheer behavioral imitation does not.

However, if mirror neuron functioning is limited to warm-blooded creatures, then not all imitation occurs in animals with mirror neurons. Red-footed tortoises copy the behavior of conspecifics: if they observe another red-footed tortoise overcome a physical obstacle by making certain moves, they become more likely to make similar moves when faced with a similar obstacle (Wilkinson et al., 2010). And then there is another factor we have not yet focused on: proximity. Various warm blooded creatures move in groups, but so too do schools of fish. And some reptiles tend to sun themselves together rather than in isolation: this is true of crocodiles and of marine iguanas. But think what this seeking of proximity amounts to. Going to the same area where others have gone or where others are is in some sense to do (approximately) the same thing that they have done. We wouldn't normally call this imitation, but in a sense, if one thinks about it, this seeking of proximity does represent a kind of primitive imitation. One may not make specific bodily movements that are similar to and imitative of the movements of others, but the location one seeks out for oneself is roughly the same as the location of other members of one's own species. And if we turn our attention from reptiles to schools of fish, the point is even clearer. When fish swim in schools they not only seek to be near one another but also, most of them, move in a direction that others in the school are moving in, and that is to imitate bodily behavior and not just location.

I am therefore inclined to believe that imitation in its most elementary forms goes back all the way to reptiles and fish and may not, therefore, depend on the existence of mirror neurons. The evolutionary advantage of mirror neurons (without empathy) would presumably then be that this allows for new forms of imitation that have survival value beyond those that occur in the absence of mirror neurons. However, not all researchers agree that mirror neurons are limited to warm-blooded species. They may, in fact, be characteristic of vertebrates generally (Miller, 2008), and I think we have a lot to learn from evolutionary neuroscientists as they further investigate issues about the evolution and functioning of mirror neurons. Mirror neurons haven't been known about for all that long, so it isn't surprising that it shouldn't be clear one way of the other at this point whether any cold-blooded creatures have mirror neurons and are capable of imitation on that basis. But whether or not reptiles and fish imitate via mirror neurons, they do imitate and they do seem to lack the more complex mirror neuron functioning that makes empathy possible. And what we have seen in any event is that imitation as such gives evolutionary advantages and that the imitation involved in empathy bestows further advantages.

Now I haven't speculated about what evolutionary benefit group sunning might have for crocodiles, marine iguanas and other reptiles, and perhaps we don't have to try to do that here, as long as we can understand the advantages of more sophisticated forms of imitation. But, in addition, I have also been assuming that empathy (as anchored in mirror neurons) involves a kind of higher-level imitation, and that is not the way that empathy is usually thought about. Associative empathy is usually regarded as a psychological mechanism whereby the states of one being are replicated in another being, and such thinking in terms of a mechanism and our very use of the term "associative" make empathy seem to be too automatic and non-behavioral to count as a form of imitation.

Similarly, when Hume in the *Treatise* (Hume, 1978) says that one person's pain can *infuse itself* into another person, he seems to be regarding the empathic process as too automatic and mental to count as a form of (even instinctual) imitation. (Hume used the term "sympathy" because the term "empathy" didn't yet exist, but he is pretty clearly talking about what we today call empathy.) But elsewhere in the *Treatise* and again speaking of what we would call empathy, Hume says that we (empathically) embrace the attitudes and opinions of other people, and the term "embrace" suggests something more active and willing that might then make it more understandable that we should think of empathy not only as a mechanism but also as a form of (typically unself-conscious) mental imitation. Empathy shows us as receptive to others and their minds, but receptivity isn't the same thing as passivity. Responsiveness is compatible with receptivity but not with passivity (in a given respect), and, in addition, someone who is receptive is *motivated to take in* what some other person has to offer. So if we think of human empathy as involving a receptivity to what others are feeling or thinking, rather than as just a kind of passivity in relation to the influence of those others, it isn't so implausible to think of it as I described it above: as a higher form of imitation directed toward other people's emotions/attitudes and not (just) toward their actions or location.

So far, then, I hope, so good. But in order to make further progress with our speculative evolutionary-psychological picture, we need to say more about the instinct for proximity. Seeking proximity is not only a primitive form of imitation, but also makes higher forms of imitation possible. Hume noticed that empathy works more effectively when the person empathized with is near to the person who empathizes, but in mirror neuron cases not involving empathy the same essential point can also be made. It is easier to imitate behavior if one sees what one is imitating, and proximity makes it possible to see and sometimes makes for *better* seeing.

But proximity also has a role in making the transmission of sympathy from mother to child occur more effectively. It is easier for babies to empathically take in the moods and emotions of those who are near to them, and the proximity via actual contact that is involved in breast-feeding ensures that a loving mother's feelings about her baby will be more empathically available to that baby than if she is merely giving the baby macerated worms with her beak. So breast-feeding not only has the advantage giving a baby food that is more ideal for it than what could come from an evolutionarily separate environment of the sort parent birds make use of to feed their babies, but also allows a mother whose child is capable of empathy to convey her feelings more effectively than would be possible with less proximate or contact-involving forms of feeding. The former advantage of lactation and breast-feeding is one all placental mammals share in, but the latter, of course, presupposes empathy, which there seems to be reason to think not all mammals are capable of. But in any event, our target of explanation is human morality based on the human mother-child relationship, and the picture is filling out now of how evolution could have gradually made human morality possible.

But at this point we also need to consider just how widely morality, as we have explained it, can be found in mammals. Only mammals seem capable of empathy, but some mammals seem to lack empathy, and we can certainly say that the latter aren't capable of morality in our terms. But what about mammals like chimpanzees and bonobos that are capable of empathy and that possess maternal instinct? Do they have morality? Well, they certainly seem capable of sympathy with one another (deWaal, 2006), and I see no reason in principle why a baby bonobo shouldn't be like a human baby in empathically taking in its mother's attitude of solicitude and becoming sympathetic with others as a result. But as I have insisted all along, this imbibed sympathy is just the (essential) foundation stone of human morality, and adult human morality clearly involves much more than that. Much of our adult human morality depends, for example, on linguistic communication between members of our species, and there is no parallel to this in other primates. However, I don't want to take on the question of whether other primates possess morality here. It is a complicated issue and one to which a great deal of literature has recently been devoted. What has more concerned us here is whether and how the foundations of human morality can be explained in evolutionary terms, and as

I conceive them, those foundations involve a transmission and teaching of empathy *on a non-verbal level*. Other aspects of morality may depend on linguistic capabilities that require evolutionary explanation(s) lying far beyond the boundaries of the present chapter. But it is difficult enough to see how even the basic foundation could have evolved, and I hope we have here said something that casts light on the very specific, but very important question.

CONCLUSION

I would like finally to mention some considerations about the evolutionary value of morality that derive from our discussion above but aren't perhaps immediately obvious in the light of that discussion. We spoke above of the value of mothering: not only with regard to the transmission of sympathy from mother to child, but also in terms of a mothering instinct that we seem to find in both cold-blooded and warm-blooded animals. There is a kind of moral value in mothering because of the seemingly selfless devotion it shows to the welfare of another creature, but we should realize that the value can be ascribed to the mothering behavior of crocodiles and other reptiles and not just to mothering among mammals and primates. No one, I suppose, is going to argue, however, that reptile mothering shows reptiles to be moral creatures—after all, they lack another feature of morality, the capacity for empathy, that is found in primates and other mammalian species that also exhibit some kind of mothering instinct. So the case for reptilian morality is a non-starter, whereas there is a real issue about whether to say that apes can be moral beings, or whether to say that they have a form of morality.

But notice that the mothering instinct in reptiles, birds, and mammals kicks in only when there are or are about to be offspring, so if mothering always constitutes some kind of (possibly very primitive) altruism, it is a form of altruism that is limited in its temporal duration and in its scope (the number and kinds of its animal "targets") as well. The maternal instinct typically focuses on the mother's own babies and not, say, the babies of others (some apes and of course humans may count as exceptions to this); and even when it focuses on the babies of other mothers, it is focused only on the very young, not on all members of the group/pack, much less on conspecifics or animals generally. However, what human and perhaps other primate mothers convey to their young offspring in the way of sympathy *isn't limited in this way*. To be sure, the loving human mother who imparts sympathy to her young child is the most naturally salient target of the sympathy that is empathically aroused in her child. But just as the anger/rage unloved and abused children feel tends to generalize and to apply itself to people other than the parents who originally caused the anger/rage (think of what serial killers and serial pedophiles do to people who never hurt or neglected them and of how people frequently vent their anger on totally innocent animals), so too does the sympathy felt by children as a result of good mothering tend to generalize. Therefore such absorbed and deeply felt sympathy tends to be much less limited in temporal duration and in the scope of its targets than anything deriving solely from maternal instinct as such.

And this generalization of altruism/sympathy depends on empathy. We can get primitively altruistic mothering and maternal instinct in animals that lack the capacity for empathy, but this constitutes a form of altruism that is limited temporally and in its scope; whereas once the capacity for empathy enters the picture, the combination of empathy with maternal instinct allows children, even babies, to develop or incorporate a generally sympathetic attitude that comes closer to the temporally and scope-wise unlimited motivation that is characteristic of morality as we know it. To be sure, empathy is partial. But so too is our morality: we think we are more obligated to help those we know and love than to help strangers. But our morality assumes that we always owe *something* even to strangers and distant others, and the possibility of such a temporally and scope-wise unlimited or less limited form of sympathy already exists, in germ, in the empathic transfer of sympathy that I have ascribed to the mother-child relationship in humans. And it exists there in a way that motherhood and maternal instinct on their own and in the absence of empathy don't seem to allow for.

Of course, many other scientist/thinkers have seen or believed in a connection between maternal/parental instinct and general human altruism/sympathy. One finds this idea in several earlier writers, including Cicero (believe it or not!) and Darwin, and more recently in the work of C. D. Batson, among others (Batson, 2011). But none of these accounts stresses the ontogenetic role of very early empathic processes in making this connection possible. The more recent discussions claim that parental instinct tends to generalize to those beyond one's own family and even one's own group, and they see childhood and adolescent concern and sympathy for others as reflecting this sort of generalization. But such approaches don't say anything very definite about why or how generalization is likely to occur, though it would be possible, I think, for them to argue that since any person or animal who needs help in a given situation resembles what babies are like almost all the time, helping those in need seems and feels very much like parenting and may thus be generally motivated along the same basic lines as parenting is.

However, there is a problem with all of this. Maternal instinct tends to be more powerful than anything fathers feel, but, as is well known, it also kicks in more strongly around the time of childbirth than at other times in a woman's or girl's life. Many girls do play at mothering dolls and may even look forward eagerly to being mothers; but is it really plausible to view all the altruistic tendencies of girls (e. g., toward lame or destitute old men and women) as connected with (eventual) mothering or parenting motivation? And can the helpfulness of boys really be explained as sourced in and a generalization from parenting instincts/motives that, unlike the case with girls, almost never specifically express themselves before the males have or are ready to have children?

Theories that regard generalized human sympathy and altruism as grounded in parental motivation need to be able to answer such questions, and I am not sure they can. But in any event these theories may not rule out what I have said about the transfer of sympathy from mother to child. And since that transfer involves parental sympathy being empathically transformed into the sympathy of someone who isn't in the position of a parent, toward certain others--e. g., the child's mother or father--who are far from being in the position of a baby or child, it should be clear that our account of how children become sympathetic with others offers a basis for generalized human altruism and empathic concern that is largely *independent* of anything that has been suggested by those who see these as rooted in parental instincts or motives that humans have from the beginning of their lives.

Batson also allows that parental neglect or abuse of a child can quash whatever tendency the child may have to sympathize with or care about others. However, my own approach not only uses empathy to explain how sympathy develops early on in children, but also emphasizes empathy (and the need for love) in explaining *how* parental mistreatment can block or undercut a child or baby's sympathy, altruism, and continued empathy--and this latter, unfortunate effect is something that approaches to altruism that rely on parental instinct have so far offered no explanation for. Perhaps, then, the two approaches could actually help each other make general human sympathy and altruism more psychologically and evolutionarily understandable. Recall too my allusion earlier in this chapter to empathic processes that Hoffman and I believe underlie the *later* moral education of children. Those who think of altruism as a generalization from parenting motives might well explain such generalization as involving these later empathic processes, and thus here too there is an opportunity for the present account and theories based primarily on parenting motivation to move closer together.

Clearly theories of sympathy and altruism that focus on parental instinct haven't highlighted empathy nearly as much as I have here. And in fact almost everything in this paper moves us toward acknowledging the great importance of empathy to human morality, an importance that has been consistently underestimated even by those who talk about empathy in their discussions of morality. However, I also hope that the speculative evolutionary arguments offered here make it possible to see how a human morality that rests, at least partly, on altruism, sympathy, and empathy can be fitted into an up-to-date naturalistic picture of the world and of ourselves (one that will or would eventually need to be integrated with results from brain science and physiology). Of course, I haven't here given you my reasons for thinking that such a natural or naturalized picture allows for moral objectivity. But we have taken on enough questions already, and I shall leave this further question to other times and other places.

REFERENCES

Batson, C. D. (2011). *Altruism in Humans*. NY: Oxford University Press.

Bowlby, J. (1952). *Maternal Care and Mental Health*. Geneva: World Health Organization.

Byrne, R. (2002). "Seeing Actions as Hierarchically Organized: Great Ape Manual Skills" in A. Meltzoff and W. Prinz, eds., *Imitative Mind: Development, Evolution, and Brain Bases*, NY: Cambridge University Press, 122-140.

de Waal, F. (2006). *Primates and Philosophers*. Princeton: Princeton University Press.

European Science Foundation News (2008). "How mirror neurons allow us to learn and socialise by going through the motions in the head." December 19.

Miller, G. (2008). "Mirror Neurons May Help Songbirds Stay in Tune". *Science*, 319, p. 269.

Hoffman, M. (2000). *Empathy and Moral Development: Implications for Caring and Justice*. Cambridge: Cambridge University Press.

Hume, D. (1978). *A Treatise of Human Nature*, ed. L. A. Selby-Bigge, Oxford: Clarendon Press.

Joyce, R. (2006). *The Evolution of Morality*. Cambridge: MIT Press.

Mealey, L. (1995). "The sociobiology of sociopathy: An integrated evolutionary model". *Behavioral and Brain Sciences*, 18, 523-599.

Milius, Susan. "The Social Lives of Snakes from Loner to Attentive Parent". *Science News* (March 27, 2004), 210.

Rochat, P. (2002). "Ego function of early imitation" in A. Meltzoff and W. Prinz, eds., *Imitative Mind: Development, Evolution and Brain Bases*, NY: Cambridge University Press.

Slote, M. (2010). *Moral Sentimentalism*. NY: Oxford University Press.

Slote, M. (forthcoming, 2013). "Egoism and Emotion". *Philosophia*.

Wilkinson, A. et al. (2010). "Social learning in a non-social reptile". *Biology Letters* 6, 614-616.

In: Psychology of Altruism
Editor: Helena Koppel

ISBN: 978-1-62808-152-7
© 2013 Nova Science Publishers, Inc.

Chapter 3

ALTRUISM AND ECONOMIC GROWTH IN AN INSTITUTIONAL THEORETICAL PERSPECTIVE

Guglielmo Forges Davanzati[*]
and Antonio Luigi Paolilli[†]
University of Salento,
Faculty of Political Sciences, Lecce, Italy

ABSTRACT

This paper aims to explore the links existing between altruism and economic growth, within an Institutionalist theoretical framework. The different notions of altruism will first be scrutinized, and the works of Thorstein Veblen and Gunnar Myrdal will be used in order to show that pro-social attitudes can play a significant role in driving economic growth, both on the supply and demand side.

Keywords: Altruism, economic growth, Institutionalism

---

[*] Email: guglielmo.forges@unisalento.it.
[†] Email: apaolilli@tiscali.it.

1. INTRODUCTION

The standard Neoclassical theory is based on the assumption that economic agents are purely rational and self-interested. This assumption is at the basis of the theory which predicts that – in the absence of external interventions – a deregulated market economy, populated by selfish individuals, tends to produce the best outcome, as regards resources allocation and economic growth. In this picture, moral norms do not play any role and the State's imposition of formal norms deriving from ethical considerations generates a sub-optimal allocation of resources and a lower growth rate than that resulting from the absence of external "interference". A classical example of this kind of reasoning lies in the minimum wage legislation, resulting from the Government's aim (or unions' aim) at improving workers' conditions, thus guaranteeing them a wage level at least corresponding to the subsistence wage. In a competitive market, on the assumption that an inverse relation between the unitary wage and employment exists, the imposition of a minimum wage produces unemployment and the consequent decline of production. Therefore, public intervention inspired by ethical considerations proves to be counterproductive, even at the expense of the groups it intends to protect. This conclusion ultimately rests on the presumed ethics or economics dichotomy (cf. Sen, 1979, 1984, 1985).

This paper sets out to show that – by contrast to the Neoclassical view – the existence (and the spread) of altruistic behaviors can be a major engine of growth. The arguments proposed are drawn from 'old' Institutionalism, with particular reference to the works of Thorstein Veblen and Gunnar Myrdal. It will be shown that altruistic behaviors – such as "workmanship" or "generosity" – can promote economic growth both on the supply and the demand side.

The exposition is organized as follows. Section 2 deals with the debate on the nature and the origin of altruism; section 3 explores Veblen and Myrdal's arguments and section 4 concludes.

2. ON THE NATURE AND ORIGIN OF ALTRUISM

Before discussing altruism and its relations with the economy we must define the term. Granted that altruism appears, however, as interest in the benefit of others, we may note that many scholars have devoted their energy to defining it and classifying the different kinds of altruism.

Khalil (2003) writes that we can distinguish three different theoretical approaches which try to answer the question *what is altruism?*: the *egoistic*, the *egocentric* and the *alter-centric approach*. The three different approaches are also related to the origin of altruism.

According to the egoistic conception of altruism (see Axelrod, 1984; Bergstrom and Stark, 1993; Taylor, 1987) altruistic behavior is determined by the expectation of future gains. The scholars who follow this line stress in fact that altruism can be *convenient* in a context of "repetitive games", above all if the games are repeated ad infinitum and provided that the expected gain for altruistic behavior is above a critical level.

This approach is obviously related to the argument that selection can favor altruism, even if it is directed to individuals with no degree of consanguinity, as long as there is reciprocity (reciprocal altruism). An important condition to permit this outcome, therefore, is that cooperation is based on prize-punishment mechanisms. Important contributions on this point are the Tit-for-Tat strategy (Axelrod and Hamilton, 1981), the Ultimatum Game, introduced by Güth et al (1982; see also Güth, 1995, and Witt and Yaary, 1992), and the Gift Exchange Game (Fehr et al., 1993). Altruism, in this context, might be the consequence of a rational choice.

However, in one particular game, the Dictator Game, in which there is a responder who can only accept or refuse the offer made by a proposer, with no consequences for the latter, it has been shown that altruism is not absent (Forsythe et al, 1994), and this is in contrast with the concept of altruism as a rational choice, drawing attention instead to genetic factors. As we will show below, the viewpoint which relates the origin of altruism to genetic factors, independently of rational behavior, can be related to the theories of *kin selection* and *group selection* and to the more recent thesis of Paolilli (2009, 2011).

For the supporters of the "egocentric approach" (Hochman and Rodgers, 1969; Becker, 1976; Dawkins, 1976), altruistic behavior is caused by the fact that the agent also considers the utility of the individuals whom he wants to benefit as a factor of his utility function. The more the latter is perceived, and therefore the more it influences decision-making processes, the more intense is the empathy level, or "emotional proximity" (depending on parental links, friendship and so on), existing between benefactor and beneficiary. In this context, Altman (2005) draws attention to the fact that neoclassical theory, which in its conventional form predicts that moral firms cannot survive in a competitive market, can incorporate the moral dimension. Using indifference curves to represent the ethical dimension in the decision-making process, Altman (2006) stresses that altruistic behavior can be compatible with a competitive market, showing, however, that economic variables remain of fundamental importance in the behavior of agents, even if they are altruists. Substantially, he underlines that "the extent of altruistic, ethical, and moral behavior simply depends on the preferences of individuals, given the economic constraints" (Altman, 2005).

Finally, the "alter-centric" approach is based on the idea that individuals tend to show pro-social behaviors, including those of pure altruism, due to the existence of a "moral gene". Unselfish behavior, according to this perspective, is based on a moral imperative which rules out rational calculation, being determined by a "natural" inclination to adopt codes of behavior marked by solidarity. Bowles and Gintis (2002), in particular, stress the role of emotions such as shame, remorse, pride, sense of guilt, which are defined "pro-social", in generating phenomena of *empathy*. The consideration of the existence of these emotions obviously places the alter-centric perspective (from an economic viewpoint) in contrast with the *mainstream* characterization of *homo oeconomicus*, self-interested and rational. Moreover, the presence of empathy and the connected pro-social emotions as the basis of social relations reduces the importance of reciprocal altruism in explaining the origin of altruism and cooperative behaviors. The alter-centric approach and, in hindsight, the egocentric approach too, are based on certain genetic characteristics of agents, which allow them able to identify with other subjects. Even reciprocal altruism probably needs, if not this *empathy*, at least the ability to anticipate emotions and actions of the others.

On the other hand it is difficult to assume reciprocal altruism as the basis of the origin of cooperative behaviors in societies made up of individuals without human intelligence, such as insects or cellular populations. The main theoretical problem that has been posed in approaching the issue of the origin of altruistic and/or cooperative behavior derives, in fact, from the general acceptance of the postulate that selection favors the strongest individuals and of the second postulate which states that altruists are the more vulnerable agents (the Darwinian paradox of survival of the altruist: Becker, 1976). It might be concluded therefore that altruism is eliminated during social evolution, which is counterfactual. Therefore many scholars have tried to explain the origin of altruism by means of other arguments, particularly that of *kin selection* and *group selection*.

The thesis of *kin selection*, or *inclusive fitness theory*, states that altruism emerges as a result of the fact that a subject's altruistic behavior is directed mainly toward his relatives. In this framework Eberhard (1975) has mathematically shown that even small degrees of consanguinity can constitute the basis for *kin selection*, and this is true, above all, with low costs for the benefactors.

This approach, however, does not explain the numerous examples of altruism directed towards strangers, collectivities, and animals and plants.

The thesis of *group selection* (Winne-Edwards, 1962), on the other hand, states that altruism involves cooperation and the internal cohesion of a group, thus favoring its survival (Sober, 1991). This thesis has been challenged by many evolutionists who think that, as the unit of reproduction in humankind is not the group but the individual, selection might favor those characteristics that maximize individual utility, thus operating against altruism. Williams (1966), in particular, argues that even if group selection is theoretically possible, its role in nature is insignificant. This happens because any level of the biological hierarchy requires a process of natural selection which operates at that level, and this is a very rare event, due to the fact that, in Williams's view, the fundamental unit of selection (the replicator, in Dawkins' terminology, 1976) is the gene. In fact, in this framework even individuals which are sexually reproducing organisms cannot be units of selection because they are not faithfully replicated.

Many scholars, however, think that genes do not totally explain altruism, and above all reciprocal altruism. Witt (1985), in particular, places importance on the capacity to learn, a capacity also referred to by Lorenz (1994 [1963]), for the animal species in general. Bergstrom and Stark (1993) believe that the behavior of an individual can essentially be determined both by genetic factors and by imitation. According to the concept of "bounded rationality" elaborated by Simon (1957, 1983, 1992, 1993), there is a gap between the actual behavior and the predictions of rational actor models. In other words, individuals are not able to maximize their objective function if the costs of information collection and processing are too great, and they therefore have a tendency to act on advice and to respect norms.

However, it cannot be denied that cultural factors, and more generally cognitive factors, are linked to a genetic substratum. Bowles and Gintis (2003 [2002]), for instance, maintain that culture and genes are strongly linked in the human species. Gintis (2000), in particular, asserts that humans show manifestations of *strong reciprocity*, which is a behavior that probably has a genetic component, because it cannot be justified only by cultural or rational motivations.

Sober and Wilson (1998) and Frank (1998, 2006), bringing *group selection* in again, have noted that, using the *Price equation* (Price, 1970), strategies that are socially beneficial but that give negative outcomes for the individuals adopting them can survive if groups dissolve and remix often enough and if there is a large covariance between traits in associated partners. This happens because groups with a high proportion of altruists have higher than average fitness and therefore grow faster than other groups, increasing the global frequency of the unselfish gene, even if its frequency falls in every group.

The multiple level of selection is therefore the central idea of the new *group selection* approach, which is based on the cognition that "there is one theory of natural selection operating on a nested hierarchy of units, of which inclusive fitness and game theory are special cases" (Wilson and Sober, 1994). In this context Bowles and Choi (2003), using an evolutionary game theory model, assert that altruism can emerge if combined with opposing sentiments (like xenophobia), due to the fact that the most cohesive groups tend to prevail in conflicts.

Finally, the thesis of *group selection*, according to Paolilli (2011), cannot explain the origin of altruism simply because the very existence of a group needs, as a precondition, the presence of cooperative aptitudes. Paolilli (2009) shows, by means of an evolutionary model, that the simplest kind of altruism (among individuals involved in binary relations) can emerge, at least initially, in a population (which is still not a group) without the concourse of the mechanisms of *reciprocal altruism*, *kin selection* and *group selection* mentioned above, and even if during their interactions, altruists do not discriminate between altruists and egoists. It is only after this stage that groups can emerge, also due to the appearance of a new kind of altruism, Benthamian altruism, directed precisely toward a group with which individuals identify (Paolilli, 2011). The interaction of this new kind of altruism with egoism (it is in fact underlined that binary relations do not disappear in human kind, since all humans are vehicles of selection, and therefore egoism cannot disappear[1]), favors the emergence of behaviors and sentiments like envy, punishment and gossip, as well as more complex social structures like nodal and hierarchical organization in teams composed of more than two individuals. In this

---

[1] Already in a previous work (Forges Davanzati and Paolilli, 2004), it is shown that the best output in a binary relation needs an equivalence between altruism and selfishness in both the agents.

perspective, altruism favors the formation of groups and the spatial concentration of the population, and this applies to all kinds of populations, from cells to humans. Kin selection, group selection and above all reciprocal altruism can contribute to evolution, but they are cofactors of it and not the prime movers.

Another major theoretical issue is connected to the relation between altruism and the market, according to two opposing links. First, it is reasonable to expect that the variation of economic variables (such as per-capita income) affects individual behavior, so that − in a context where intrinsic motivations are of a pro-social nature - the increase in per-capita income *makes it possible* for these motivations to be expressed in actual pro-social behaviors. Second, the opposite effect is likely to occur, so that the occurrence of altruistic behavior can itself modify economic variables, with particular reference to the growth rate. The next section will address this topic, with reference to the 'old' Institutionalist theoretical framework[2].

3. INSTITUTIONS, ALTRUISM AND ECONOMIC GROWTH

This section ll explore the effects of the spread of altruistic behavior on economic growth, based on the Institutional view that the rational choice paradigm cannot explain the numerous motives which mould agents' behavior (cf. Hodgson, 1988). While economists and sociologists have devoted much attention to the role of habits, customs, power relations and "instincts" in criticizing the rational choice paradigm on Institutional bases, little attention has been devoted to the idea − which is clearly present in the 'old' Institutional tradition (Veblen and Myrdal, above all) − that economic agents also behave according to pro-social motives, and that this can drive economic growth. As will be shown, pro-social behavior can drive economic growth both on the supply side and on the demand side. Schematically, the first view can be attributed to Thorstein Veblen and his theory of the "instinct of workmanship" and the second to Gunnar Myrdal and his theory of "rational generosity". This approaches will be examined separately.

1) *Thorstein Veblen and the "instinct of workmanship".* Veblen assumes that individual's decisions are affected by "instinct", to be conceived as historically and socially affected and not as purely biological variables. The

---

[2] So by contrast a decline of per-capita income should render individual *behavior* more selfish, even when their *motivation* is altruistic.

"instinct of workmanship" – hereafter IW - is typical of "technicians", and involves their desire to fully exploit their scientific knowledge[3]. It is closely linked to what Veblen calls "idle curiosity", which concerns the desire for knowledge as an end itself. As Veblen clarifies, when it is in operation and in a long-term perspective, the IW produces "the most substantial achievement of the race – its systematized knowledge and quasi-knowledge of things" (Veblen, 1964 [1914], p.87).

O'Hara (2000) shows that the instinct of workmanship falls within the Veblenian category of "good instincts", i.e. instincts which "promote the collective welfare or collective life process of the global society". Similarily, Asso and Fiorito (2004, p. 448) distinguished between "other-regarding and self-regarding instincts. The former have as their aim the welfare of the family, clan or group, while the latter find expression in aggression, predation, and domination"[4].

The full application of the IW in the production process significantly contributes to economic growth, insofar as it is connected with the genesis and the spread of innovation[5]. In Veblen's view, innovations basically manifest by means of a reduction of technical capital turnover, thus generating increases in hourly labor productivity. If technical progress does not produce mass technological unemployment, the sole positive effect it produces is the possibility – on the part of firms – to exploit economies of scale, thus generating an increase in production (Smith, 2002). This line of thought leads to the conclusion that *the more the instinct of workmanship is exploited, the higher the rate of economic growth becomes.* It is worth noting that – according to Veblen – the instinct of workmanship falls into the realm of pro-social attitudes, in the broader sense. In other words, technicians are not interested in increasing their firms' profits, but they are mainly interested in promoting social well-being. Accordingly, this type of 'altruistic' behavior is

---

[3] This "instinct of workmanship", besides a broad kind of altruism, can be related to what Jantsch (1980) defines as the aim of "pure intensification of life". In his words, in fact, "if the drive of evolution were simply adaptation, then evolutionary change should have ceased with the bacteria" because they are able "to mutate and adapt to all kinds of adverse conditions with amazing speed", while instead it seems that what men and, more generally, living creatures pursue is not only mere survival, but also and perhaps above all the "pure 'intensification of life'" (the phrases in inverted commas are from Briggs and Peat (1989, p. 155).

[4] Good instincts include also what Veblen labels "parental bent", related to care of other people.

[5] To Veblen, the full exploitation of innovation deriving from the work of technicians is prevented by "businessmen" aiming to obtain profits by reducing output and increasing prices – so-called "industrial sabotage". This issue falls outside the scope of this section. See, among others, Forges Davanzati (2006).

to the advantage of all members of the society, insofar as it is the basis of a growth mechanism operating on the supply side.

2) *Gunnar Myrdal and "rational generosity"*. Myrdal examines the issue of rational generosity in dealing with the free-riding problem and, specifically, in addressing the problem of tax payment:

> "When people are better off and have great security they feel freer to give up privileges and to let down barriers which keep others out and are more prepared to carry the costs of the common burden. And this process, in turn, strengthens the foundation for continuous economic progress" (Myrdal, 1957, p.40)[6].

This argument rests on the following implicit assumptions:

i)   agents are inclined to behave altruistically, and the increase in their income is *at least* a condition allowing altruistic behavior to occur;

ii) the 'degree' of morality encapsulated in individual action is not independent of the variations of economic variables.

Reasoning within a Keynesian theoretical framework, Myrdal (1957; 1958) stresses that the increase in public expenditure – mainly in the form of expansion of the Welfare State – raises the employment rate. He adds that wages rise as employment increases: "a rise in employment will almost immediately raise some levels of living" (Myrdal, 1957, p. 20). The rationale for this argument lies in the fact that, as employment increases, workers' bargaining power grows too, thus producing a wage increase. It is interesting to observe that- according to Myrdal – workers' struggle for wage rises is above all a struggle for power and social and moral recognition, and should be regarded from the standpoint of social psychology. He clarifies this issue in his *Political elements in the development of economic theory* (Myrdal, 1951 [1930], p.119) "The demands for higher wages, shorter working time, etc. are,

---

[6] Myrdal does not develop this argument, which is highly relevant to the contemporary debate in ethical economics, and the effects of pro-social attitudes (such as altruism) on economic development. His argument is important, since it challenges the dominant view supporting the free-riding theory: it is intended to show that free-riding behaviour is not invariant with respect to both income distribution and the Institutional and social setting. By means of behavioral experiments, Bowles and Hwang (2012) have recently shown that hostility towards opportunism and social pressure aimed at lowering purely selfish attitudes are likely to overcome the problem of free-riding, thus generating a state where the individual contribution to the production of public goods is not nil.

of course, important in and of themselves, but viewed more deeply, they are only an expression of far more general strivings for power and demands for justice on the part of a social class which simply feels oppressed. Even if there were no hope of forcing through higher wages, the battle would go on. Even if the workers had reason to believe that a decline in productivity and wages would result, they would nevertheless demand more power and codetermination in the conduct of business. In the last analysis, more is at stake for them than money; their joy of labor is involved, their self-esteem, or, if one will, their worth as men. Perhaps no great strike can be explained merely as a strike for higher wages".

On the basis of these assumptions, the following sequence holds.

- An increase in public expenditure generates an increase of employment and production;
- the increase in employment produces an increase in wages;
- due to the "rational generosity" argument, the increase in wages is associated with a higher propensity to pay taxes, thus generating a cumulative process of economic growth where public expenditure becomes even more self-financed.

In view of this sequence, economic growth is proportional to the individual propensity to co-operate, due to a self-enforcing mechanism of increasing per-capita income – increasing tax revenues – increasing public expenditure, operating on the demand side (see Forges Davanzati and Paolilli, 2004).

These arguments lead to the following basic comment: the occurrence of altruistic behavior is not independent of economic growth, and altruism can be both the cause and the effect of variations of both economic growth and income distribution (cf. Forges Davanzati, 2006).

CONCLUSION

This paper deals with the effects of altruistic behavior on economic growth. A preliminary critical reconstruction of the nature and origins of altruistic behavior has been presented. Moving within the Institutional theoretical framework – with particular reference to the works of Veblen and Myrdal – it is argued that the existence (and the spread) of altruistic propensities can promote economic growth, both on the supply and on the demand side. This occurs due to the operation of the Veblenian "instinct of workmanship" and of the "rational generosity" effect, as theorized by Gunnar Myrdal.

REFERENCES

Altman, M. (2005). Reconciling altruistic, moralistic, and ethical behavior with the rational economic agent and competitive markets. *"Journal of Economic Psychology"*, 26, 732–757.

Altman, M. (2006). Opening-up the objective function: choice behavior and economic and non-economic variables-core and marginal altruism *"Economics Bulletin"*, 4 (33), 1–11.

Asso, P. F. and Fiorito, L. (2004). Human nature and economic institutions: Instinct psychology, behaviorism, and the development of American institutionalism, *"Journal of the History of Economic Thought"*, vol.26, n.4, pp.445-477.

Axelrod, R., Hamilton,W. D. (1981). The evolution of Cooperation, *"Science"*, 211 (4489), 1390–1396.

Axelrod, R. (1984). The Evolution of Cooperation, New York: Basic Books.

Becker, G. S. (1976). Altruism, egoism, and genetic fitness: economics and sociobiology, *"Journal of Economic Literature"*, 14 (3), 817–826.

Bergstrom, T. C., Stark, O. (1993). How altruism can prevail in an Evolutionary Environment, *"The American Economic Review"*, 83 (2), 149–155.

Bowles, S., Choi, J.-K. (2003). The Co-Evolution of Love and Hate, Università degli Studi di Siena, Quaderni, p. 401.

Bowles, S., Gintis, H. (2002). Prosocial emotions, working paper, 2, Santa Fe Institute.

Bowles, S., Gintis, H. (2003 [2002]). The Origins of Human Cooperation, in Peter Hammerstein (Ed.), *Genetic and Cultural Evolution of Cooperation*, MIT Press, pp. 430–443.

Bowles, S. and Hwang, S-Ha (2012). Is altruism bad for cooperation?, *"Journal of Economic Behavior and Organization"*, 85, pp.330-341.

Briggs, J., Peat, F. D. (1989). Turbulent Mirror: An Illustrated Guide to Chaos Theory and the Science of Wholeness, New York: Harper & Row Publishers.

Dawkins, R. (1976). The Selfish Gene, New York: Oxford University Press.

Eberhard, M. J. W. (1975). The evolution of social behavior by kin selection, *"The Quarterly Review of Biology"*, 50, 1-33.

Fehr, E., Kirchsteiger, and G., Riedl, A. (1993). Does fairness prevent market clearing? An experimental investigation, *"The Quarterly Journal of Economics"*, 108, 437-459. doi:10.2307/2118338.

Forges Davanzati, G., and Paolilli, A. L. (2004). Altruismo, scambi e sviluppo economico, in L. Tundo Ferente (Eds.), La responsabilità del pensare, Napoli: Liguori Editore, 289-307.

Forges Davanzati, G. (2006). Ethical codes and income distribution. A study of John Bates Clark and Thorstein Veblen, London-New York: Routledge.

Forsythe, R., et al. (1994). Fairness in simple bargaining experiments, *"Games and Economic Behavior"*, 6, 347-369.

Frank, S. A. (1998). Foundation of Social Evolution, Princeton: Princeton University Press.

Frank, S. A. (2006). Social selection, in Fox, C. W.,Wolf, J. B. (Eds.), Evolutionary Genetics: Concepts and Case Studies, New York: Oxford University Press, pp. 350–363.

Gintis, H. (2000). Strong reciprocity and human sociality, *"Journal of Theoretical Biology"*, 206, 169-179. doi:10.1006/jtbi.2000.2111.

Güth,W., Schmittberger, R., Schwarze, B. (1982). An experimental analysis of ultimatum bargaining, *"Journal of Economic Behavior and Organization"*, 3 (4), 367–388.

Güth, W. (1995). On ultimatum bargaining experiments-a personal review, *"Journal of Economic Behavior and Organization"*, 27, 329- 344. doi:10.1016/0167-2681(94)00071-L.

Hochman, H., Rodgers, J. (1969). Pareto optimal redistribution, *"American Economic Review"*, 4, 542–557.

Hodgson, G. (1988). Economic and institution. A Manifesto for a modern institutional economics, Cambridge/Oxford: Polity Press and Basil Blackwell.

Jantsch, E. (1980). The Self-Organizing Universe: Scientific and Human Implications of the Emerging Paradigm of Evolution, Oxford – New York: Pergamon Press.

Khalil, E. L. (2003). What is altruism?, *"Journal of Economic Psychology"*, 1, 97-123.

Lorenz, K. (1994). L'aggressività, Milano: Il Saggiatore. Italian translation of Das sogenannte böse: Zur naturgeschichte der aggression (1963), Wien: Verlag.

Myrdal, G. (1944). An American dilemma: the negro problem and modern democracy, New York.

Myrdal, G. (1957). Economic Theory and Underdeveloped Regions, London: General Duckworth & Co.

Myrdal, G. (1958). Beyond the welfare state. Economic planning in the welfare states and its international implications, London: Methuen.

Myrdal, G. (1968). Asian Drama: An Inquiry into the Poverty of Nations, New York: Pantheon.

Myrdal, G. (1969). Objectivity in social research, New York: Pantheon.

O' Hara, P. A. (2000). Marx, Veblen, and contemporary institutional political economy, Cheltenham: Elgar.

Paolilli, A. L. (2009). About the "economic" origin of altruism, *"The Journal of Socio-Economics"*, 38, 60-71.

Paolilli, A. L. (2011). Altruism, Selfishness and Social Cohesion, *"Sociology Mind"*, 2011, Vol. 1, n. 4, pp. 199-204.

Price, G.R. (1970). Selection and covariance, *"Nature"*, 227 (5257), 520–521.

Sen, A. (1979). Utilitarianism and welfarism, *"Journal of Philosophy"*, n. 76, pp. 463-480.

Sen, A. (1984). Resources, Values and Development, Oxford: Blackwell; Cambridge: Harward University Press.

Sen, A. (1985). Goals, Commitment, and Identity, *"Journal of Law, Economics, and Organizations"*, n. 1 (2), Fall, pp. 341-355.

Simon, H. A. (1957). Models of man: Social and rational, New York: Wiley.

Simon, H. A. (1983). Reason in human affairs, Stanford: Stanford University Press.

Simon, H. A. (1992). Bounded rationality and the cognitive revolution, Elgar: Aldershot.

Simon, H. A. (1993). Altruism and economics, *"The American Economic Review"*, 83, 156-161.

Smith, M. (2012). Demand-led growth theory: A historical approach, *"Review of Political Economy"*, vol.24, n.4, pp.543-573.

Sober, E., Wilson, D.S. (1998). Unto Others: Evolution and Psychology of Unselfish Behavior, Cambridge, MA: Harvard University Press.

Sober, E. (1991). Organisms, individuals, and units of selection, in Tauber, A.I. (Ed.), Organism and the Origins of Self, Dordrecht, Netherlands: Kluwer, pp. 275–296.

Taylor, M. (1987). The Possibility of Cooperation, Cambridge: Cambridge University Press.

Veblen, T. B. (1899a). The theory of the leisure class, New York: A. M. Kelley, 1975

Veblen, T. B. (1899b). Mr. Cummings's strictures on "The theory of the leisure class", *"The Journal of Political Economy"*, vol.8, n.1, December, pp.106-117.

Veblen, T. B. (1892). Böhm-Bawerk's definition of capital and the sources of wages, *"Quarterly Journal of Economics"*, vol.6, Jan., pp.247-252.

Veblen, T. B. (1904). The theory of business enterprise, New York: A. M. Kelley, 1965.

Veblen, T. B. (1905). Credit and prices, *"The Journal of Political Economy"*, vol.13, n.3, June, pp.460-472.

Veblen, T. B. (1906 [1901]). Industrial and pecuniary employments, in *"The place of science in modern civilization and other essays"*, pp.279-323.

Veblen, T. B. (1908). On the nature of capital: Investment, intangible assets, and pecuniary magnate, *"The Quarterly Journal of Economics"*, 23, 1, pp.104-136.

Veblen, T. B. (1910). Christian morals and the competitive system, *"International Journal of Ethics"*, vol.20, n.2, January, pp.168-185.

Veblen, T. B. (1919). The vested interests and the state of the industrial arts, New York: B.W.Heubsch.

Veblen, T. B. (1920). Review of John Maynard Keynes, The economic consequences of the Peace, *"Political Science Quarterly"*, pp.467-472.

Veblen, T. B. (1921). The engineers and the price system, Kitchener: Batoche Books, 2001.

Veblen, T. B. (1923). Absentee ownerhip and business enterprise in recent times. The case of America, New York: B.W.Huebsch.

Williams, G. C. (1966). Adaptation and Natural Selection: a Critique of Some Current Evolutionary Thought, Princeton: Princeton University Press.

Wilson, D. S., and Sober, E. (1994). Reintroducing group selection to the human behavioral sciences, *"Behavioral and Brain Sciences"*, 17, 585-654. doi:10.1017/S0140525X00036104.

Winne-Edwards, V. C. (1962). Animal Dispersion in Relation to Social Behaviour, New York: Hafner.

Witt, U. (1985). Imagination and leadership—the neglected dimension of an evolutionary theory of the firm, *"Journal of Economic Behavior & Organization"*, 35, 161–177.

Witt, U., and Yaary, M. (1992). An evolutionary approach to explain reciprocal behavior in a simple strategic game, in U. Witt (Eds.),

Explaining process and change — Approaches to evolutionary economics (pp. 23-34), Ann Arbor: University of Michigan Press.

INDEX

genes, 61
genetic factors, 59, 61
genocide, 36
God, 4, 24, 34
grounding, 17
growth, viii, 57, 58, 63, 64, 66, 67, 69
growth mechanism, 65
growth rate, 58, 63
growth theory, 69
guilt, 60

H

hedonism, 17, 30, 32
helping behavior, 11, 12, 16, 27, 34
history, 11, 12, 18, 19, 31, 34, 44, 45
horses, 46
hostility, 65
hotel, 3, 27, 28
human, vii, 2, 5-9, 18, 19, 22-29, 31-35, 37-
    41, 44, 45, 47, 49-54, 60-62, 68-70
human actions, 29
human behavior, 18, 22, 70
human cognition, 7, 9
human existence, 25
human experience, 23, 29
human motivation, 19, 40
human nature, 8, 18, 19, 33
humanistic psychology, 32
hypothesis, 11, 43

I

ideal, 39, 50
ideals, 22, 39
illusion, 24
imitation, viii, 37, 47, 48, 49, 55, 61
income, 63
income distribution, 65, 66, 68
independence, 21
indifference curves, 60
individual action, 65
individualism, 19
individuals, 22, 25, 29, 47, 58-62, 69

information processing, 9
insects, 60
instinct, viii, 37, 45, 47, 49-54, 63, 64, 67
institutional economics, 68
integrity, 28
intelligence, 7, 60
intentionality, 32
interference, 58
intervention, 31, 58
intrinsic motivation, 63
isolation, 48
issues, 6, 10, 16, 38, 39, 40, 48

J

Jews, 3, 4, 5, 13, 24, 27, 34, 35
jumping, 8

K

Keynes, 70
Keynesian, 65
kicks, 51, 53
kin selection, 59, 60, 61, 62, 68

L

lactation, 45, 50
language acquisition, 10
laws, 21
lead, vii, 1, 42, 66
leadership, 70
learning, 33, 55
legislation, 58
leisure, 70
lens, 29
light, 17, 19, 28, 51
love, 17, 18, 33, 34, 42, 43, 45, 52, 53
lying, 20, 51

M

machinery, 17